—LOST LINES—
LIVERPOOL
and the
MERSEY

NIGEL WELBOURN

Ian Allan
PUBLISHING

Contents

ISBN 978 0 7110 3190 6

Published by Ian Allan Publishing

an imprint of Ian Allan Publishing Ltd, Hersham, Surrey, KT12 4RG.
Printed in England by Ian Allan Printing Ltd, Hersham, Surrey, KT12 4RG.

Code: 0804/B2

Visit the Ian Allan Publishing website at www.ianallanpublishing.com

Cover photographs courtesy of Colour-Rail

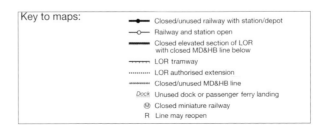

Key to maps:

- ●—— Closed/unused railway with station/depot
- —○—— Railway and station open
- ——— Closed elevated section of LOR with closed MD&HB line below
- Τ┰Τ┰Τ LOR tramway
- ·········· LOR authorised extension
- ┈┈┈┈ Closed/unused MD&HB line
- *Dock* Unused dock or passenger ferry landing
- Ⓜ Closed miniature railway
- R Line may reopen

Introduction

Merseyside has a unique and rich railway history. The first inter-city railway, together with the first overhead electric, underwater and inter-urban electric railways in the world were to be found here. Innovation was at the forefront of the growth of railways in the area. Liverpool became the supreme example of a commercial port at the height of Britain's Empire. The area became a gateway to the world, and the stimulus for this came from the railway links to the Mersey quaysides. The railway beneath the River Mersey provided the impetus for further growth on the Wirral peninsula, and an equally extensive railway network developed on the Birkenhead side of the Mersey, together with docks and shipbuilding industries.

A trip on the Liverpool Overhead Railway, prior to World War 2, would have unfolded views of the massive dock complex below. It would have also provided an insight to Britain's history at the height of its power. There were references to Empire in the names of many stations on the line from Canada to Nelson.

Decline of the railways came over many years but accelerated after World War 2 and resulted in a reduction in the number of lines serving Merseyside. The 1963 Beeching Report into the reshaping of the then nationalised British Railways proposed extensive passenger cuts in the area.

The economic decline, particularly in the 1960s and 1970s in the Mersey docks, was reflected in a declining and uncertain railway network serving the area. Coal from British coalfields, once the main fuel of railways, ships and industry, was replaced by other fuels. The Mersey docks have undergone considerable change and rationalisation, the rail-served warehouses and labour-intensive dock-transfer methods have gone, and new shipbuilding is no more, all of which has resulted in the loss of many freight lines, sidings and industrial buildings.

Yet there are many astonishing reminders of lost lines, including some fantastic early remains, still to be found. Equally there were sensible reprieves, and many of the draconian cuts proposed by the Beeching Report were never implemented. In 1997 the first private operator took over Merseyrail. Talk is now of extending the electric services, adding new stations and reopening passenger services, the possibilities including Edge Hill–Bootle, St Helens Junction–St Helens and the North Mersey branch from Aintree to Bootle. The area has reinvented and reinvigorated itself, and an excellent railway network still serves Merseyside. Many dock areas are revitalised, while the River Mersey and its ferries remains as alluring and as lively as ever.

Right: Underneath the Overhead. An ex-LYR 'Pug' 0-4-0ST, No 51253, dating from 1901, belches steam and smoke onto the Liverpool Overhead Railway structure, despite the chimney cowl designed to redirect its smoke. The photograph was taken near James Street station on 22 October 1955. *P. Kelly*

1 First and Last

The Merseyside area is unique for world railway 'firsts'. As far back as 1830 the Liverpool & Manchester Railway became the first main line in the world, the first to be operated entirely by steam engines, the first to have double track, the first to run to a timetable and the first to operate with its own stock — in short, the world's first modern railway. While on the opening day William Huskisson, the MP for Liverpool, became the first person in the world to be killed by a passenger train, the railway was a huge success. By 1837 Liverpool was linked to Birmingham and by 1850 to an extensive railway network that served the coalfields, cotton towns and industries, all of which in turn assisted the prominence of Liverpool as a port. At the height of the British Empire Liverpool, Birkenhead and the River Mersey became a key area for trade with the rest of the world.

The pioneering nature of the area did not end here. In 1833 the first rail-to-ship facility was opened at Runcorn Gap, while in 1873 the first gravity-worked goods yard opened at Edge Hill. In 1886 the first deep-level urban underground railway was opened beneath the River Mersey; it later became the first underwater railway to be electrified, in 1903.

Meanwhile, 1893 had seen the opening, in Liverpool, of the world's first elevated electric railway. The Liverpool Overhead Railway boasted the first station escalator, at Seaforth Sands, and the first automatic signalling, and later the line became the first to employ two-aspect colour daylight signals. The first inter-urban electrified service ran from Liverpool to Southport, some trains running by March 1904. All these innovations provided an unrivalled level of railway service at the time.

On the Wirral peninsula was Birkenhead, the first town in Britain to have trams, the first line opening in 1860. This area developed with its famous shipbuilding yards, which were responsible for many marine 'firsts'. Birkenhead Docks were seen as a threat to Liverpool's, and in 1857 the two were merged to form the Mersey Docks & Harbour Board, the first public trust in Britain.

The rival railways all saw great opportunities in the Merseyside area. The LNWR and LYR became dominant in the Liverpool area, but there was also the CLC, formed of representatives of the GCR, GNR & MR. On the Wirral peninsula the Birkenhead Railway provided the GWR with access to the Mersey, and the GCR provided a link to Bidston.

The Wirral, Mersey and Liverpool Overhead railways developed as more local lines, but altogether a well-developed network served the area. However, proposals in 1901 for a 110mph electric monorail linking Liverpool with Manchester did not proceed.

All the main railways aimed to provide a competitive edge over their rivals. Sleeping cars were introduced in 1875, by both the LNWR from Liverpool Lime Street to Euston and the Midland Railway from Liverpool Central to St Pancras. The GWR provided corridor trains from Paddington to Birkenhead in 1892 and made extensive use of the Mersey ferries from Birkenhead to Liverpool.

After the 1923 Grouping Liverpool appeared on the maps of three of the 'Big Four' railway companies then created. The GWR reached the Mersey via Birkenhead Woodside, and the LNER was able to reach the area via the CLC and ex-GCR lines, but the LMS became the main railway to serve the area.

There was a decline in the docks during the 1920s and 1930s, but World War 2 was to see extensive use of all the transport facilities for the war effort. During the war Merseyside became the prime target after London, and devastating air raids caused enormous destruction. In May 1941 seven consecutive nights of air raids resulted in every railway from Liverpool being blocked for a while. There were many acts of bravery by railway staff in the Merseyside area, and several received honours from King George VI.

After the war all the railways in the area were in a run-down condition, and nationalisation of the railways came in 1948. The LOR was not included in the nationalised network as it was considered a separate local passenger route. The dock lines of the MD&HB were not included as part of the BR network, although railway docks and shipping were brought under Government control.

Apart from the extensive rail-borne freight traffic provided by trade through the docks, until the 1950s all ships using the docks, including the great ocean liners, ran on coal, and many needed refuelling by coal trains. The area also dealt with railway exports; for example, the largest station roof in South America, at Buenos Aires, was dispatched from Garston. Locomotives were exported from the Vulcan Foundry at Newton-le-Willows, although American locomotives, to help the World War 2 effort, were for a time imported through Birkenhead Docks.

Some closures date from the earliest times, and in 1836 Liverpool Crown Street became the first major passenger station in the world to close. However, significant decline of the railways began with the diminishing of the Mersey's marine trade, particularly after World War 2. The economic decline was reflected in the population of the area. Liverpool's population is still only about half what it was in the 1930s, the decline being greater than in any other British city. This has been reflected in the use of the railways, the Garston branch closing to passengers in 1947 and the Alexandra Dock service the following year. In 1956 the LOR became the first electrified urban railway in Britain to close.

Yet it was the 1963 Beeching Report, described as 'drastic and disastrous' for the area, that really threatened to decimate the railway network. Despite recognising that Liverpool relied on a daily influx

5

of rail commuters, it went on to propose closure of intermediate stations on the erstwhile L&MR, of the electrified ex-LYR coast route to Southport, the ex-LYR route to Manchester, all lines to St Helens, the ex-GCR line to Bidston on Wirral and sections of the ex-BJR and ex-CLC routes.

The 1960s was not a good time for the railways in the area, and the lack of investment is apparent from the following extract from the author's diary of September 1967:

An old dog with a collection box on its back was seen at Crewe. Particularly dirty coaches were noted on the line to Ormskirk, lots of old lamps were seen stored at the very quiet Woodside station, and a steam tank engine was noted in poor condition at Liverpool Exchange.

There were many closures, and even the Mersey ferries came under threat. There were also some sensible reprieves, including the electrified ex-LYR Liverpool–Southport service, the two Liverpool–Wigan lines, the Bidston–Wrexham route and several stations on the erstwhile L&MR. However, Liverpool Exchange and High Level Central stations, together with Birkenhead Woodside, were closed, and sadly all had their great iron trainsheds demolished. There was also considerable rationalisation of track and facilities on remaining lines.

The history of Merseyside is integrally linked with railways. It is generally recognised that the last regular BR steam-hauled passenger express train arrived at Liverpool Exchange on 3 August 1968, and a commemorative 'farewell to steam' special

Above right: The first daytime colour-light signalling, on a permanent basis, was introduced on the LOR, the signals being seen here after their installation in 1921. The line also had the first electrically operated automatic train-stop system, the apparatus for which can be seen at the bottom right-hand corner of this view towards the Pier Head station and Royal Liver Building. The LOR closed in 1956, and the bridge seen here was demolished in 1958. *Ian Allan Library*

Right: The Liverpool Exchange–Southport Chapel Street route was generally recognised as the first substantial inter-urban electric service in Britain, opening in 1904. An ex-LYR electric baggage car, in LMS livery, is seen at Liverpool Exchange on 19 October 1946. Built in 1921, this vehicle represented the last addition to the LYR's electric stock. *H. C. Casserley*

Right: The railways' first freight depot to serve Liverpool docks was at Wapping. At the time of its opening access was by the longest double-track tunnel in the world. This view, recorded on 5 November 1960, features MD&HB 0-4-0PT No 4 (on the left) and an ex-LYR 'Pug' 0-4-0ST, No 51206 (right), the latter in its final week of service. The depot itself would close to rail traffic in 1965. *L. Sandler*

departed from Lime Street on 11 August 1968. Yet the railways have survived remarkably well, and their decline, like that of Merseyside itself, has been reversed. Rail-borne freight has returned to Liverpool Docks, and the new link and loop lines under Liverpool were the first underground railways to be built in the 20th century outside London. The area's fortunes continue to revive, its resurgence being evident from the well-used and modernised railway network. At last it is not just the past that Liverpool relishes but, for the first time in many years, the future as well.

Below: One of the last regular BR steam express workings was the Liverpool Exchange– Glasgow Central service, seen here leaving Exchange station behind 'Black Five' 4-6-0 No 44858 on 29 April 1967. The Beeching Report proposed diverting long-distance trains to Lime Street station and closing the electrified line to Southport. *P. Gerald*

Right: The last train from Liverpool Central High Level station, a DMU for Gateacre, departs on Saturday 15 April 1972. Losses for that year were estimated at £150,000, prompting Merseyside PTE to withdraw the service and close the station. *J. Cadman*

Right: Class 31/1 No 31 248, in Railfreight livery, leaves Birkenhead Docks on 22 July 1988 with the daily trip working to Warrington. In 2008 the track at this location remained *in situ*, albeit heavily overgrown; indeed, such was the undergrowth that since 1993 (when the freight line was last used) it had reached the top of the retaining wall seen in the background. *R. Cragg*

Right: The 14.45 for Paddington — the last passenger service to be worked by the last ex-LMS 'Crab' 2-6-0, No 42942 —waits to depart Birkenhead Woodside station on 31 December 1966. Birkenhead–Paddington trains were the last in the British Isles timed to run at an average speed of more than 60mph with steam traction.

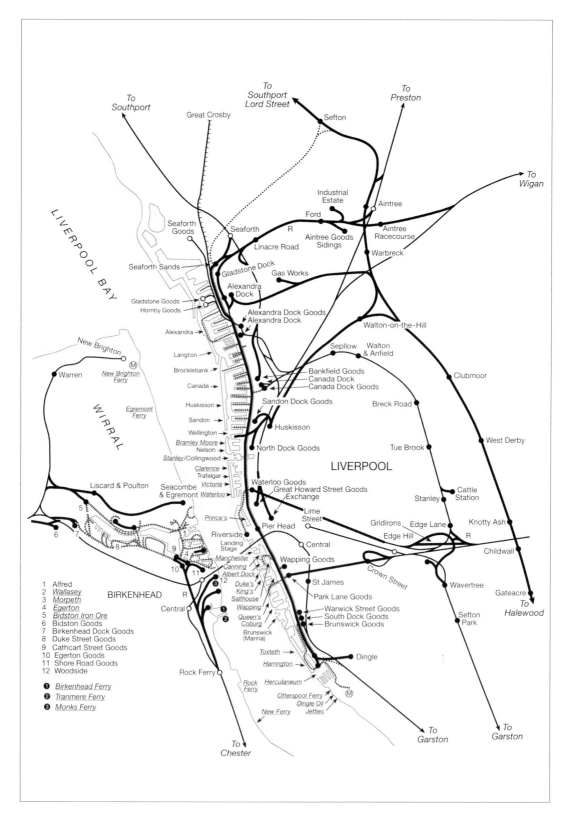

To Southport

To Southport Lord Street

To Preston

To Wigan

Great Crosby

Sefton

Aintree

Industrial Estate

Ford

Aintree Goods Sidings

R

Aintree Racecourse

Warbreck

LIVERPOOL BAY

Seaforth Goods

Seaforth

Linacre Road

Seaforth Sands

Gladstone Dock

Gas Works

Alexandra Dock

Gladstone Goods
Hornby Goods

Alexandra Dock Goods
Alexandra Dock

Walton-on-the-Hill

Alexandra

New Brighton

New Brighton Ferry

Langton

Brocklebank

Canada

Seplow

Walton & Anfield

Clubmoor

Bankfield Goods
Canada Dock
Canada Dock Goods

Breck Road

Warren

WIRRAL

Egremont Ferry

Huskisson

Sandon

Wellington

Bramley Moore

Nelson

Stanley/Collingwood

Clarence

Trafalgar

Victoria

Waterloo

Sandon Dock Goods

Huskisson

North Dock Goods

LIVERPOOL

Tue Brook

West Derby

Liscard & Poulton

Seacombe & Egremont

Waterloo Goods
Great Howard Street Goods
Exchange

Stanley

Cattle Station

5

Prince's

Lime Street

Gridirons

Edge Lane

Knotty Ash

6   7

8

9   4

10   11

Riverside

Landing Stage

Manchester

Canning

Albert Dock

Duke's

King's

Salthouse

Wapping

Queen's

Coburg

Brunswick (Marina)

Pier Head

Central

Wapping Goods

St James

Park Lane Goods

Warwick Street Goods
South Dock Goods
Brunswick Goods

Edge Hill

Crown Street

Wavertree

R

Childwall

Gateacre

To Halewood

BIRKENHEAD

Central

R

3   12

1

2

Rock Ferry

Toxteth

Harrington

Herculaneum

Dingle

Sefton Park

Rock Ferry

Otterspool Ferry

Dingle Oil

New Ferry

Dingle Oil Jetties

To Chester

To Garston

To Garston

1   Alfred
2   Wallasey
3   Morpeth
4   Egerton
5   Bidston Iron Ore
6   Bidston Goods
7   Birkenhead Dock Goods
8   Duke Street Goods
9   Cathcart Street Goods
10 Egerton Goods
11 Shore Road Goods
12 Woodside

❶ Birkenhead Ferry
❷ Tranmere Ferry
❸ Monks Ferry

2 A geographical perspective

The River Mersey, from its beginnings near Stockport, flows some 70 miles past Warrington, Runcorn, Liverpool, Birkenhead and New Brighton to form a wide estuary into the Irish Sea at Liverpool Bay.

The silting up of the River Dee helped the port of Liverpool to develop, but it was the pioneering dock technology that kept the port ahead of competitors. Development was also undertaken on the Wirral peninsula, and links across the Mersey were one of the main geographical problems to be overcome. At Runcorn a railway crossing opened in 1869, while the Mersey railway tunnel opened in 1886.

The Industrial Revolution required good port facilities, and all the railways in the Mersey hinterland were able to reach the main docks on the River Mersey. Liverpool grew to become the second port of the Empire and as a point of emigration to America. It was crucial for the export of products from the industrial North, notably the Lancashire cotton towns, and the Midlands. Other areas along the Mersey waterfront were also to develop as rail-served ports, including Bromborough Port, Ellesmere Port, Runcorn, Widnes, Garston and Birkenhead in particular. By 1900, on both sides of the Mersey, there were almost 90 docks, including more than 20 dry docks, and about 36 miles of quay.

The St Helens Canal had provided impetus for a rival railway, while the Manchester Ship Canal was strongly opposed by the LNWR. The ship canal opened in 1894 and allowed ocean-going ships to reach Manchester. It begins with locks off the Mersey at Eastham and passes Ellesmere Port and the Stanlow Oil Refinery on its 36-mile route to Manchester.

Part of Liverpool's urban area was built on an outcrop of sandstone, which had to be cut or tunnelled through to reach the banks of the Mersey. By its peak in 1931 Liverpool's population had reached 855,539, and the city had developed as an important port for transatlantic passenger traffic to America. Although this is no more, Liverpool is still a very significant sea port and, due to its location on the west coast, remains important for Irish and American trade.

On the Birkenhead bank shipbuilding was once important, and over the years Cammell-Laird built a wide range of vessels. At one time live cattle were also imported in huge numbers from Ireland. By 1931 Birkenhead's human population had reached 147,946. Rural Wirral developed as residential suburbs for Liverpool and Birkenhead, while the large villas of Victorian merchants were also to be found on the coast towards Southport, and both localities provided seaside amenities for the industrial areas.

Elsewhere St Helens was once an industrial centre for coal mining and is still famous for the manufacture of glass. Parts of the counties of Lancashire and Cheshire surrounding the River Mersey became well known as Merseyside, and in 1974 this was formally recognised as the Metropolitan County of Merseyside; the book broadly covers this and much of the Merseyrail area.

Right: A map of the ex-LYR network on tiles at Manchester Exchange station, showing the extensive ferry services from Liverpool and running powers on the Lancashire bank of the River Mersey, seen in February 2005. *Author*

Left: Map showing closed lines in the Liverpool and Birkenhead area.

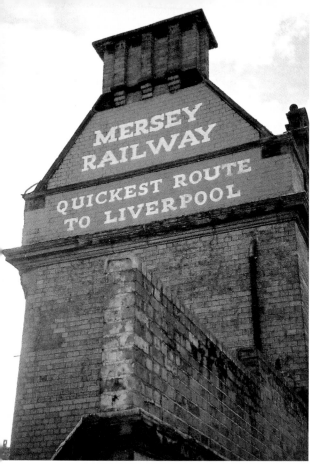

Above left: A Royal charter to operate a ferry service between Liverpool and Birkenhead was granted in 1330, but crossing the Mersey Estuary underground was a major geographical obstacle that was first overcome by the Mersey Railway in 1886. Birkenhead Central station, seen here in September 2006, is still open and still extols the virtues of the Mersey Railway. *Author*

Above: Viewing the Mersey by use of the LOR and LYR, as shown on this simplified map of the Lancashire coast. The poster includes Captain's Lane station (later Ford), which opened in 1906, and the name (pasted over that of an earlier manager) of Mr Neachell, who joined the LOR in 1908, giving a guide to its date of publication. It shows the through connections between the LYR and LOR, which after an initial period became very limited. It also reveals that many of Liverpool's railways were on a north–south alignment because of the sandstone outcrop. *Ian Allan Library*

Left: A bridge on the ex-CLC route near West Derby, photographed in September 2006. It was built to span four tracks; the sandstone, a key geological feature of this area, would have been removed had the line ever been quadrupled. However, while freight traffic to the docks was extensive, two tracks were all that was required. Eventually singled, the line had fallen out of use by 1975 and was officially abandoned in 1979. *Author*

③ The lost tunnels

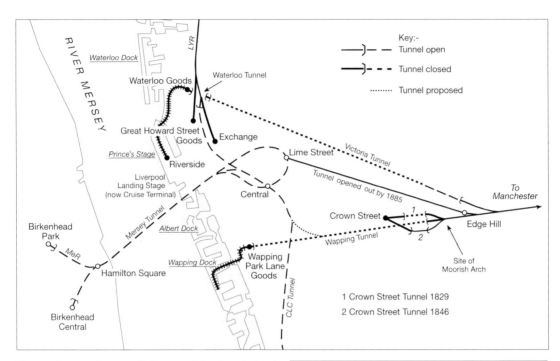

Key:-
- ─────)─ ─ ─ Tunnel open
- ─────)─ - - - Tunnel closed
- ········· Tunnel proposed

1 Crown Street Tunnel 1829
2 Crown Street Tunnel 1846

Above: Map of tunnels under Liverpool.

The grain merchants of Liverpool having joined with the cotton merchants of Manchester to overcome opposition, the Liverpool & Manchester Railway opened to passengers in September 1830 and to freight in December. This was the world's first real commercial inter-city railway, and passengers and freight were welcomed.

The Liverpool end of the line was complicated by a sandstone outcrop, and in order to avoid disruption to existing city areas tunnels were required. At Edge Hill the cutting eventually led into three tunnels with adjoining portals. They mainly had brick-arched roofs, with part-brick but also exposed-sandstone side walls. The first led to Liverpool Crown Street station; this tunnel was designed by George Stephenson and had a date stone of 1829. Crown Street soon became inadequate for the growing passenger traffic and was also some way from the city centre, in part because Liverpool Corporation had been somewhat reluctant to accept steam locomotives. The station closed to passengers in August 1836, when Lime Street station opened, thereby becoming the first major passenger terminus in the world to close.

The original single-track tunnel was 291yd long and built to relatively modest dimensions, about 12ft (3.7m) high and 15ft (4.6m) wide, as it was designed for operation solely with rope-hauled passenger coaches. Consequently, on the opening of the more convenient Lime Street, the former passenger station at Crown Street was connected to Edge Hill by a second, larger tunnel and by 1846 was in use as a goods depot and coal yard. By 1972, following the cessation of all traffic to Crown Street, the later tunnel was used as a head shunt from Edge Hill yard, while the original tunnel of 1829, which had been used for freight, closed.

Although passengers became important, freight was also the intended traffic of the L&MR line, and the links from Edge Hill to the docks had a profound effect on the history of Merseyside. The Wapping Tunnel, from Edge Hill to Wapping goods depot (renamed Park Lane Goods by the LMS), was 1 mile 351yd in length. Constructed between 1826 and 1829, it opened in September 1830, at which time it was the world's longest double-track tunnel.

Wapping Tunnel was of larger dimensions than the original Crown Street Tunnel, being more than 17ft (5.2m) high and about 22ft (7m) wide.

Above: 'The Tunnel', from an Ackermann print, published in 1831. The print was drawn by T. Bury and engraved by H. Pyle and shows a rope-hauled freight train descending in the gas-lit Wapping Tunnel. The original print, showing a steam locomotive hauling the train, had to be amended because it was inaccurate; close inspection reveals that the first wagon has a pair of suspiciously large wheels! *Liverpool Record Office, Liverpool Libraries*

Left: The site of the Moorish arch and engine house on 18 March 1979. Evidence of the early L&MR construction is still visible, including the engineer's stairs and boiler house set into the cutting side; also the sunken rope-haulage system at track level. The historic site was opened to the public for a time in connection with the 'Rail Trail' between Edge Hill and Crown Street for the 'Rocket 150' celebrations in 1980. *R. Foster*

It descended from the Edge Hill cutting to Wapping at a 1 in 48 grade. Charles Vignoles and Thomas Gooch (brother of Daniel) were both involved with the construction of the tunnel. During construction the tunnel threatened the foundations of houses in St Georges Square, and other surveying errors were such that Vignoles was forced to resign, the work being completed by Joseph Locke. Near Wapping the tunnel roof was later made up of girders supporting the CLC tunnel between Liverpool Central and St James. The double-track Wapping Tunnel was originally designed for use by rope-hauled freight; consequently, as steam locomotives were not used, it was initially provided with gas lights and was whitewashed. Locomotives were first used in 1896. The goods depot at Park Lane closed in 1965, and the tunnel fell out of use.

Above: A scene recorded on 8 April 1979, from near the site of the Moorish arch, at Tunnel Road, Edge Hill. The tunnels seen are, from left to right, the 'new' 1846 tunnel to Crown Street, built from an extension of a dead-end tunnel workshop, the 1829 Wapping Tunnel to Wapping goods depot and the original 1829 Stephenson's tunnel to the Crown Street passenger terminus, which is just visible. *R. Foster*

Right: The same location in September 2006. The 'new' Crown Street Tunnel, seen on the left, had been cleared of debris and used as a head shunt for revived dock traffic. The dimensions of Stephenson's original single-line Crown Street Tunnel, right, were quite small. *Author*

Joseph Locke and George Stephenson were also involved with the construction of the adjoining Victoria and Waterloo tunnels, which together provided a second link from Edge Hill to the Mersey at Waterloo Dock. The Victoria Tunnel, from Edge Hill to near Waterloo Dock, was 1 mile 946yd long. It was built for two tracks, had a gradient of 1 in 60 and was the largest of the tunnels, being about 18ft 3in (5.6m) high and 26ft (7.9m) wide. The tunnel opened in August 1849. Opened at the same time, the Waterloo Tunnel is a similar but separate tunnel, being some 852yd in length, although the two tunnels are more widely known collectively as the Waterloo Tunnel. Originally freight was rope-hauled, but the two adjoining tunnels went over to locomotive haulage and dockside tracks were extended to Riverside station in 1895, when the tunnels were first used for passenger traffic. The tunnels fell out of use in March 1971.

The original tunnels to Liverpool Lime Street (construction of which uncovered a labyrinth of earlier, non-railway subterranean rooms and tunnels) were initially also designed for cable haulage. From 1870 locomotives were used, but the climb to Edge Hill resulted in the tunnels' being very smoky, and some accidents happened, and consequently they were for the most part widened to the current four-track cutting.

Although the early tunnelling from Edge Hill to Crown Street and the docks is out of use, such was the construction of these tunnels that they are likely to remain extant for a very long time, and sporadically plans for reuse are considered.

Left: Crown Street's passenger services ended in August 1836, but the site remained in use until 1972 as a coal yard. When this view was recorded, on 8 April 1979, tracks had been removed, and the area was being landscaped. The ventilation chimney for the Wapping Tunnel, below Crown Street, is prominent. To its right can be seen Stephenson's original 1829 Crown Street Tunnel, which was blocked off upon completion of the landscaping scheme in 1980. The larger 1846 Crown Street Tunnel can just be seen in the distance. *R. Foster*

Below left: Stephenson's original Crown Street Tunnel of 1829 had mostly unlined walls, except where faults were encountered in the sandstone, and a vaulted brick roof. The single-line tunnel was used until the final closure of Crown Street goods depot and remains extant today. In spite of the stalactites, the interior is still in good condition in this September 1998 view, which also shows well the gradient of the line. *N. Catford*

Below: A ventilation chimney at Crown Street, for the Wapping Tunnel below, photographed in September 2006 from a position close to the top of the original Crown Street Tunnel entrance. The chimney was added when steam trains first used the tunnel. A commemorative plaque to mark the 175th anniversary of the opening of the railway on this site was unveiled in September 2005. *Author*

Right: The current western portal of the Wapping Tunnel, seen on 29 October 2006. Although rather unimposing, as changes were made as the depot was expanded by the LNWR in 1864 and after it was closed by BR, it was perhaps this tunnel in particular that in 1830 changed the history of Merseyside, for the first time providing rail access to Liverpool's docks. Liverpool's importance as a commercial port and its contribution to the Industrial Revolution were largely based on the success of the railway. *Author*

Below: The Wapping Tunnel was a very ambitious project for its time, being cut on a gradient through solid rock, with brick arching and some brick lining where layers of wet clay were exposed. This interior view was recorded in September 1998, after rail use had ended and the track had been removed. *N. Catford*

Left: Additional ventilation shafts, needed to clear the smoke from steam locomotives (which had replaced rope haulage), were added to the Victoria Tunnel in the years 1897-9. The chimneys for these are surprisingly varied. This one, photographed in September 2006, has been extended in length. Several of the chimneys were originally surrounded by buildings. *Author*

Below: A short section at the eastern end of the Waterloo Tunnel was used as a headshunt for Edge Hill Yard, as seen here from the platform of Edge Hill station in September 2006, but by this time most of the tunnel was disused. The western portal of this tunnel, off Pall Mall, is also still extant, as is a substantial bridge carrying ex-LYR freight lines near the tunnel's western extremity, where a Liver Bird has been carved into a stone lozenge. *Author*

4 The Liverpool Overhead Railway

As Liverpool's docks developed, congestion in the area became acute, and an overhead railway appeared to provide the best answer to prevent further overcrowding on the teeming dock-road entrances. In 1888 work eventually began on an elevated double-track railway that was about 16ft above road level. From the very beginning this was an innovative undertaking, large mobile structures being used to erect the multitude of standard metal spans and bridges that were built on steel stanchions above the roads and railways along the route.

Steam could not be used due to the fire risk from cinders to the ships' cargoes below, many of which were combustible, and the weight of locomotives would have required a more substantial and expensive elevated structure. The Chairman of the LOR, Sir William Forwood, had studied electric railways in America, and the courageous (for the time) and pioneering decision was taken to use electricity. Consequently the LOR became the first electrified elevated railway in the world, the 500/525V DC being supplied originally by a coal-fired generating station, which was located beneath a viaduct on the LYR dock branch.

The Prime Minister, Lord Salisbury, conducted the opening ceremony in February 1893, almost six years after construction began, and the following month the first section, from Herculaneum Dock to Alexandra Dock, opened to the public. The Alexandra Dock–Seaforth Sands extension was opened in April 1894, the Herculaneum–Dingle section following in December 1896 to give a 6½-mile line, almost continuously on a viaduct along the Mersey waterfront. The electric trains worked well, and throughout its lifetime the LOR provided a reliable service.

There were some notable engineering features on the route. At Bramley-Moore Dock the line was forced to dive under the LYR branch that was used to supply ships' coal. This was known as the 'switchback', the steepest gradient taking the LOR under the LYR being 1 in 40. Elsewhere on the route there were swing and bascule bridges, while the final ½-mile section at Dingle involved a tunnel, providing the odd experience of the overhead railway being underground!

Although attractive to visitors, whose sightseeing interests extended to viewing shipping from all parts of the world, the line primarily provided access for workers in the dockland area. At first it did not prove the success that was hoped for, but the northern and southern extensions to the original line into suburban areas added to its success as a commuter railway. A further link to the LYR, from Seaforth Sands, opened in July 1905, and until 1914 through trains were run by the LYR to and from Southport. Originally the electric current on the LOR was conveyed by a central rail, with return through the wheels, but the connection with the LYR electric system required an outside live rail and the use of dual-voltage stock.

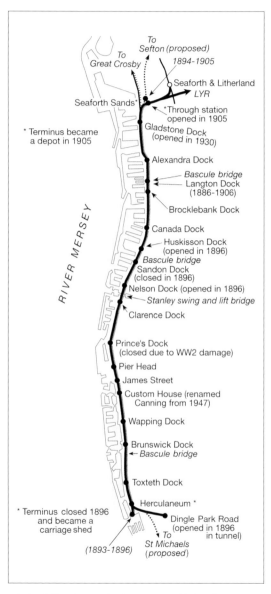

To Sefton (proposed) 1894-1905

To Great Crosby

Seaforth & Litherland LYR

Seaforth Sands*

*Through station opened in 1905

* Terminus became a depot in 1905

Gladstone Dock (opened in 1930)

Alexandra Dock

Bascule bridge
Langton Dock (1886-1906)

Brocklebank Dock

RIVER MERSEY

Canada Dock

Huskisson Dock (opened in 1896)

Bascule bridge
Sandon Dock (closed in 1896)

Nelson Dock (opened in 1896)

Stanley swing and lift bridge

Clarence Dock

Prince's Dock (closed due to WW2 damage)

Pier Head

James Street

Custom House (renamed Canning from 1947)

Wapping Dock

Brunswick Dock
Bascule bridge

Toxteth Dock

Herculaneum *

* Terminus closed 1896 and became a carriage shed

Dingle Park Road (opened in 1896 in tunnel)

To St Michaels (proposed)

(1893-1896)

The railway was the first to install automatic signalling. An arm on the track was struck by the train and activated an electric current that in turn activated an electromagnet, which automatically set the semaphore signal behind the train to Danger; the signal was not cleared until the train had reached the next station and block section. This system reduced considerably the number of signalboxes required on the line, and only two were regularly manned. Long-range day colour-light signals, installed by Westinghouse, replaced the semaphores in July 1921 and again were the first of their type in Britain.

Plans in the 1920s for further extensions, from Seaforth Sands to Sefton and from Herculaneum Dock to St Michaels, to provide a circular electric route via the CLC Hunt's Cross–Southport line, did not proceed, and longer-distance through trains were never developed.

Left: The northern terminus of the LOR at Seaforth Sands opened in April 1894, when the line was extended from Alexandra Dock. The first railway-station escalator was installed here in 1901. The two covered platforms of the original, mainly wooden terminus are seen after connection had been made with the LYR in 1905. The railway was extended to this terminus to tap into the surrounding residential district. A connecting railway-owned tram service to Great Crosby was introduced in 1900. *Ian Allan Library*

Right: Seaforth Sands became a through station in July 1905, when the line was extended further, to the LYR Seaforth & Litherland station. The escalator, which had caused some problems with long dresses, was removed. A full service commenced in 1906, but, although through trains ran to Southport, complete integration with the LYR was never achieved. The station was damaged by an arson attack in 1956 and although temporarily repaired was demolished after closure late in 1957. *Ian Allan Library*

Below: The bascule bridge at Sandon Dock in the raised position. The rolled-steel decking can be clearly seen, as can the pylons that supported the telegraph and electricity cables spanning the gap. The bridge allowed large loads, of over 14ft in height, to pass under the LOR and gain access to the dock area. Most of the standard structures built for the LOR were prefabricated in the nearby LYR freight yard. Other bascule bridges on the line were to be found at Brunswick and Langton docks. Whenever possible they were raised at night, to minimise disruption to the railway. *Ian Allan Library*

Above right: The 'switchback' under the LYR high-level coal branch at Bramley-Moor Dock. The 1-in-40 and 1-in-80 gradients under the bridge are apparent at this point on the LOR, which followed the dockside for most of its route and was therefore subject to few other significant changes in gradient. *Ian Allan Library*

Right: The unique double-deck swing and lift bridge at Stanley Dock epitomised the remarkable engineering of the LOR. This view shows the structure being 'weight proofed' with stock, probably just prior to the opening of the line. It also shows the scale of the two moving sections, the LOR being on the upper level and MD&HB freight lines at the lower level. The design, approved in 1891, included lifting sections on the lower level that could be raised without disrupting the LOR; for larger ships the whole bridge could be swung open. *Ian Allan Library*

Left: The Stanley Dock swing and lift bridge viewed from the north *c*1900, with the south swing leaf in the 'off line' position. The swing bridge, together with the adjoining road lifting bridge, allowed sailing ships access to Stanley Dock and interchange with the Leeds & Liverpool Canal. The MD&HB goods lines, under the passenger-only LOR, are apparent in this view. *Ian Allan Library*

Below left: The Pier Head station platforms. The original central live rail was gradually removed once connection with the LYR system, in 1905, required an alternative outside live rail to be fitted. This was the busiest station on the LOR, particularly with dock workers travelling from Liverpool city centre to the north dock stations. The platforms were covered, and each had its own stairway to street level. Unusually for the LOR, ticket facilities were provided at street level. *Ian Allan Library*

Below: James Street Bridge in the 1920s. The 'layered' building in the background, built in 1898, was once the headquarters of the White Star Line. The sinking of the *Titanic* was announced from balconies of the besieged building in 1912. *Ian Allan Library*

Right: The LOR was a pioneering and individualistic railway of worldwide renown and a noted Liverpool institution. Installed by Westinghouse, the long-range two-aspect colour-light signals seen here — the first in Britain — were brought into use on 27 July 1921. *Ian Allan Library*

Below: The Herculaneum carriage shed occupied the site of the original Herculaneum station, which was the original southern terminus of the LOR, until the line was extended to Dingle in 1896. This photograph, with the approach to Dingle Tunnel on the left, was taken towards the end of the railway's life. *Ian Allan Library*

Bottom: Adjoining the Dingle Tunnel portal was a 200ft-long iron lattice girder bridge, seen here in the 1950s. Plans for a further LOR station in this area, to connect with the CLC below, did not proceed. *Ian Allan Library*

5 A day on the Dockers' Umbrella

Although the Liverpool Overhead Railway was often described as simply 'the Overhead' (or 'Ovee') it became more well known as the 'Dockers' Umbrella'. Although freight lines ran directly beneath it, most were set in cobbles and allowed pedestrian access to the docks. Thus the waterproof overhead structure, designed to prevent anything from falling onto those beneath, provided an ideal shelter for many of the thousands of dockers in Liverpool, most of whom prior to 1949 lived on low wages and had no guaranteed work. Consequently they mainly walked to work, often underneath the railway, which acted as a convenient 'umbrella' in wet weather, and indeed it was not unknown for some even to sleep under the structure.

The iconic overhead railway also lent the Liverpool waterfront very much an American atmosphere. This was reinforced by the fact that many of the electric trains ran in a three-car formation, as per contemporary American practice, while the 'Three Graces' had features reminiscent of New York's early skyscrapers.

In the years before containerisation the docks were labour-intensive, and many workers used the LOR to commute, the large number of closely spaced stations and the frequency of trains indicating the intensity of the railway's operations. It was also used by the city's white-collar workers, and First-class accommodation was provided. Tourists wishing for a bird's-eye view of the bustling docks below also began to use the line, and by 1919 about 18 million passengers a year were travelling on what had become a well-loved and popular railway.

There was stiff competition from the trams, which were subsidised by Liverpool Corporation, but the overhead railway offered a faster service. In 1902 the journey time over the line was accelerated to 22 minutes to provide the fastest stopping service in the world. However, the additional power and maintenance costs of this service led to trains' being decelerated by 6 minutes over the route in 1908. By way of recompense the frequency of trains was increased, such that they ran every three

Left: A classic view of the iconic LOR. By 1913 the railway had 51 passenger coaches. Originally 15 twin-car sets were used. A third coach was introduced to the sets from 1895, but they could not be run in multiple. One of the original coaches is seen here having just left James Street station in the 1950s. Viewed from the outside, the driver's cab was on the right, and passenger seating was provided on the left. *A. Porter*

Below: The LOR timetable of April 1910 provided frequent trains from 4.45am until 11.33pm, a service unrivalled in the country at that time. The timetable is taken from Bradshaw's guide, which was established by George Bradshaw, a Lancashire printer.

SEAFORTH and DINGLE.—Liverpool Overhead.
Gen. Man. and Eng., E. J. Neachell.

Seaforth Sands to Dingle (Park Road) every 5 minutes from 4 45 mrn. to 6 aft., then every 10 minutes to 11 33 aft.   SUNDAYS, every 10 minutes from 11 3 mrn. to 11 23 aft., and 11 30 aft.
Seaforth and Litherland (L. & Y.) **to Dingle** (Park Road) every 10 minutes from 5 30 mrn. to 11 30 aft.   SUNDAYS at 11 30 mrn., and every 10 minutes from 12 10 noon to 11 20 aft.
Dingle (Park Road) **to Seaforth Sands** every 5 minutes from 5 mrn. to 6 30 aft., then every 10 minutes to 11 30 aft.   SUNDAYS, every 10 minutes from 11 mrn. to 11 30 aft.
Dingle (Park Road) **to Seaforth and Litherland** (L. & Y.) every 10 minutes from 5 mrn. to 11 10 aft.   SUNDAYS at 11 mrn., and every 10 minutes from 11 40 mrn. to 10 50 aft.
☞ The Trains call at Alexandra 3, Brocklebank 5, Canada 7, Huskisson 8, Nelson 10, Clarence 11, Prince's 14, Pier Head 17, James Street 18, Custom House 19, Wapping 21, Brunswick 22½, Toxteth 24, Herculaneum 26, and arrive at Dingle 28 minutes after leaving Seaforth Sands.
Clarence, Custom House, and Toxteth Stations are closed on Sundays.

Right: The LOR loading-gauge could not accommodate the 10ft-wide Liverpool–Southport electric stock, so special stock was built by the LYR at Horwich. Here a two-coach train for Southport stands at Pier Head station. The through service ran during summer months from 1906 until the outbreak of World War 1. *B. Horne*

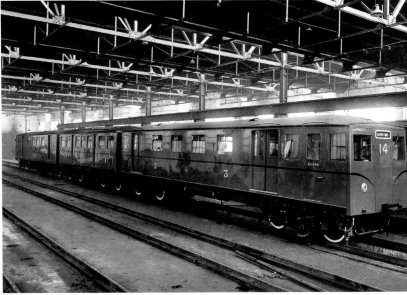

Below right: In 1946 work began on rebuilding the original wooden coach bodies in a lightweight aluminium alloy. The modernised coaches had pneumatically operated doors and eight sets were in operation by 1955. The first modernised carriages, Nos 14, 7 and 30, are seen here in the shed at Seaforth Sands after the end of World War 2. No 7 survives today. *Ian Allan Library*

Below: The interior of a First-class coach with high-backed seats. Although leather upholstery was originally provided, and window blinds were added for the World War 2 blackout, there were no luggage racks, and even in these coaches 'Spitting Prohibited' notices were displayed. Other features incuded mirrors, pictures of ships and advertisements. *Ian Allan Library*

minutes at peak times. Between 1932 and 1935 an express service operated on Sundays, but otherwise trains called at all stations.

At its peak the port of Liverpool could be host to about 100 ships at any one time, but the economic depression of the docks in the 1920s and '30s saw a decline in shipping and consequently the number of passengers using the line. Attempts to improve passenger receipts were made by advertising, and in 1932 particularly cheap fares were brought in to encourage travel. Also introduced were tourist tickets that on occasions additionally allowed visits to ocean liners in the docks. Even with somewhat reduced patronage all looked set fair, but insufficient investment on repair and maintenance of the metal structure was to lead to the LOR's eventual downfall.

Left: Third-class coaches were more basic, with wooden seats. However, when the coaches were rebuilt in an aluminium alloy, low-backed upholstered seats were provided in bays of six, with two seats facing inward to the central corridor. 'Hanging straps' for busy times replaced the poles, while the opening door windows gave way to opening top-lights. *Ian Allan Library*

Right: The only steam locomotive operated by the LOR was *Lively Polly*, an inside-cylinder 0-4-0WT built by Kitson of Leeds in 1883 for the West Lancashire Railway. Acquired in the 1890s, it gave many years of service on permanent-way trains. It was sold in 1949 to Rea Ltd, a coal merchant in Birkenhead, and ended its days handling coal trains on the Monks Ferry branch. This view shows well its de-icing scraper shoe. *Ian Allan Library*

Below: Alongside *Lively Polly* in the shed at Seaforth Sands in 1948 was a Ruston diesel purchased the previous year. The steam locomotive was probably out of use by this time, the distinctive LOR central coupling having been transferred to the diesel, which nevertheless retained standard buffers. *Ian Allan Library*

Above: A distant view, recorded in the 1950s, of Seaforth Sands depot, which occupied the site of the original station terminus. Also to be seen are the signals from the mainly goods dock lines below. *Ian Allan Library*

Right: The distinctive two-tone brown livery as applied to the ends of rebuilt coaches Nos 1, 18 and 24. The photograph was taken in the early 1950s at the Seaforth Sands depot, which had itself been rebuilt in 1926. *A. Porter*

Left: Gladstone Dock station opened in 1930 to serve the enlarged dock complex and was the last station to be added to the LOR. It was on a restricted site and backed onto the LMS North Mersey goods depot. Only the northbound platform had access to street level, and consequently this was the only LOR station with two footbridges, which allowed entry to and exit from the southbound platform. *Ian Allan Library*

Right: A view of Gladstone Dock station, showing how well used this station once was by dockers, ship repairers, seafarers and office workers. A considerable covered seating area was provided, but platform facilities were fairly basic. The photographs of Gladstone Dock are undated, but the apparent lack of new stock suggests the late 1930s. *Ian Allan Library*

Left: The LOR ran some 274 trains a day in the 1930s, its use being encouraged by extensive advertising. This poster features a vessel at almost every berth. Note that Mr Neachell's name has been removed, dating it to after 1926, when his term of office ended. *Ian Allan Library*

Above right: A train headed by rebuilt coach No 5 leaves Clarence Dock station on 14 May 1956. The station served the Stanley and Trafalgar docks and was very busy. *J. Davis*

Centre right: LOR timetable, July 1955.

Below right: Most LOR trains ran in a standard three-car formation, the middle car having been added to cope with increased patronage. Many coaches remained in original form until the end; unrebuilt Nos 9 and 10 are seen entering James Street station on 13 October 1956 *A. Porter*

Below: Huskisson Dock station, opened in 1896 as a replacement for Sandon Dock station, plays host to a school party *c*1950. A trip on the railway served as an ideal geography and history lesson for local schoolchildren, who looked forward to seeing the ships from the vantage-point of the LOR, and special trains could be arranged. The station has long gone, but the dock, named after the local MP killed by the *Rocket*, survives. *Ian Allan Library*

Table 8   **SEAFORTH and DINGLE—Liverpool Overhead—6½ miles**

Frequent Service—MONDAYS to FRIDAYS, 6 24 a.m. to 10 3 p.m.   SATURDAYS 6 24 a.m. to 10 3 p.m.   SUNDAYS 7 0 a.m. to 10 3 p.m.
Closed Sundays:—§¶ Gladstone, Canada,   ‡¶ Nelson, James Street,   ¶ Wapping and ¶ Toxteth,
‡ Also at 6 30 p.m., approximately Mondays to Fridays   § Also at 7 5 p.m. on Mondays, Tuesdays, Wednesdays and Fridays at 6 30 p.m. on Thursdays
¶ And at 2 30 p.m. approximately on Saturdays.
Huskisson closed at 2 30 p.m. approximately on Saturdays.
Intermediate Stations at Gladstone, Alexandra, Brocklebank, Canada, Huskisson, Nelson, Clarence, Pier Head, James Street, Canning, Wapping,
Brunswick, Toxteth and Herculaneum.

Top: A Custom House–James Street train photographed in the late 1930s. Liverpool's elegant Custom House would be destroyed during World War 2, the station consequently being renamed Canning in 1947. In the background can be seen the 'Three Graces', all destined to survive the war. That furthest away is the Liver Building; dating from 1911, it has the largest clock mechanism in Britain, while the rooftop Liver Birds stand some 18ft tall. *Ian Allan Library*

Above: Canning station in the 1950s, with stock rebuilt with smooth aluminium-alloy exterior leaving for Dingle. Most stations provided similar facilities, but the rebuilt Canning station had mainly covered platforms. *Ian Allan Library*

Left: The damage caused by air raids during World War 2 is apparent in this view of the patched-up overhead structure. Wood was often used for wartime repairs as an alternative to steel, which was in short supply. The MD&HB goods railway ran under the LOR for almost its entire length. It may also be noted that the overhead structure, which provided about 14ft headroom, was in reality one long metal bridge that was expensive to support and maintain. *Ian Allan Library*

⑥ The lost Umbrella

Sandown Dock station was the first to close, in 1896, Langton Dock station following suit in 1906, but otherwise the LOR operated without significant interruption until World War 2, when it suffered significant damage. In May 1941 air raids brought down the overhead line at Canada, Canning and Wapping docks, blocking the freight lines below. The damage and disruption was so severe that consideration was given to closing the railway, and the LMS even agreed to employ displaced staff. However, the fact that, during the war years, about 14 million passengers annually were still using the line ensured that it was quickly repaired, although damage to Prince's Dock station was so extensive that it never reopened.

Below: North of Gladstone Dock station four trainsets await their fate in 1957, after closure of the LOR. A massive effort was put into saving the line, and following its closure hopes of a revival delayed scrapping of the remaining 54 coaches, but much of the stock had been broken up by the end of 1957. *Ian Allan Library*

After World War 2 the Liverpool Overhead Railway was one of the few urban lines that escaped nationalisation in 1948, mainly because it was a self-contained private railway that carried only passengers. However, these twin facts now made the line vulnerable. Postwar changes to the dock trade meant less labour as messengers were replaced by telephones, bulk cargoes required less docker handling, and the decline in the number of vessels meant a reduction in crews, repairs and maintenance, all resulting in a drop in patronage of the LOR. Compounding the situation, the trams reduced their fares to compete.

Being effectively on a metal viaduct for almost its entire route, the LOR needed more maintenance than did a conventional line. A full-time maintenance team was employed, but repairs did not keep pace with what was really required, with the result that, by the 1950s, repair costs were rising. Over the years parts of the elevated decking had been allowed to become superficially rusty, and, whilst this did not affect the soundness of the structure, in the mid-1950s severe corrosion was discovered on some

sections of the elevated rolled-metal deck plates. This had been caused not so much by the sea air but by the soot from dock locomotives, which operated directly below the metal structure; although chimney cowls were used, these were only partly effective, and the mixing of soot with rainwater formed a corrosive acid that attacked the ironwork. The occasional blocked drain did not help, while the rusting of the decking under the rails had been exacerbated by grit and the vibration of the trains. An independent firm of consulting engineers recommended complete replacement of the decking within five years. It was soon realised that funds were insufficient to provide for this work. Consequently the independent LOR asked Liverpool Corporation, the MD&HB and BR for help with the £2 million required for repairs to keep the line open.

The LOR was not some little-used branch line but a busy, electrified urban commuter route. Moreover, thousands made use of the railway for pleasure at weekends, and at this time almost 9 million passengers annually were still being carried on the line, which was still returning a profit for its shareholders. Yet in February 1955 the first rumours of closure appeared in the local press.

Strenuous efforts to arrange a takeover or mount a rescue bid proved unsuccessful. Liverpool Corporation, which operated competing services, was unwilling to help, nor was BR prepared to take over the line. Public meetings were held, but closure notices were posted, and, despite massive protest, the line was closed on 30 December 1956. The last two regular passenger trains, packed to the gunnels, were timed to pass at Pier Head, where, amidst noise of detonators, the crowds gave them a rousing send-off.

At the time of closure it had been agreed that the line would be left intact for nine months. Come September 1957, with growing vandalism of the disused stations and stock, it was recognised that a rescue bid would not be forthcoming. The scrap merchant duly moved in on 23 September, and by January 1959 demolition of the railway was complete.

The line has not entirely fallen into oblivion, stanchions at Wapping having been incorporated into a wall, while at Stanley Dock the foundations of the double-deck swing bridge remain. The subterranean terminus still exists at Dingle, as does the Dingle tunnel portal at Brunswick, and bricked-up doorways are to be found in the dock wall to Huskisson station. As for the rolling stock, one of the original wooden electric cars has been preserved, and a rebuilt First-class aluminium-alloy coach survives, while the atmosphere of the overhead railway will be recreated at the new Museum of Liverpool, scheduled to open in 2010.

The LOR has been the only heavily used and extensive stretch of urban electric railway to be lost in Britain. The grimy and snaking structure, striding above the docks, had great character and afforded wonderful views over Liverpool's bustling docks, while the names of its stations — Nelson, Brunswick and Canada —epitomised Britain's greatest global influence. Its loss is perhaps best summed up by the prophetic words of the LOR's last General Manager: 'The time will come when Merseysiders must rue the day when they permitted the City Fathers to throttle the lifeblood of this unique undertaking and in addition scrap the last vestige of their remarkably efficient tramway system.' It will long be remembered with affection.

Left: Breaking up the stock at Seaforth Sands carriage sheds began in July 1957, and partly dismantled coaches are seen here in a sea of debris. This was the main depot on the line, although the old station at Herculaneum was also used to store carriages for peak-hour services. *Ian Allan Library*

Above right: Dismantling of the LOR structure began on 23 September 1957. This photograph shows the early stages of demolition, involving the removal of a section of the elevated decking near Pier Head. The width of the structure seen here was 22ft, and it was estimated that altogether there were about 80 acres of metal decking to be removed. In the background stands Liverpool's parish church of St Nicholas. After closure of the LOR few people other than the dockers themselves ever saw the docks again. *Ian Allan Library*

Right: Demolition of the bowstring girder bridge near the Pier Head was difficult and was left until last, as is evident from this view recorded prior to July 1958. The art-deco obelisk on the left is the ventilation shaft for the Mersey road tunnel. *Ian Allan Library*

Left: All the metal was destined for scrap. Oxyacetylene cutters rendered sections into 'furnaceable' lengths, seen here being loaded near James Street, at the rear of the 'Three Graces'. George Cohen & Sons was awarded the demolition contract, which stipulated that demolition be effected by May 1959, but in fact the work was largely complete by January of that year. *Ian Allan Library*

Left: The semi-circular pit and pivot seating for the double-deck swing and lift bridge at Stanley Dock remain, this photograph being taken in October 2006. Here coastal vessels could link with the Leeds & Liverpool Canal, but the relatively narrow dock entrance led to a gradual decline in this traffic, while the freezing up of the waterway during the winter of 1962/3 brought an end to its commercial use. *Author*

Above: LOR hand-lamp.

Above right: The southern extension and tunnel to Dingle was cut through sandstone and opened in December 1896. The tunnel was almost half a mile long. This view of the entrance portal, which was restored for the International Garden Festival, was recorded in April 2006. *Author*

Far left: Behind closed doors: one of two blocked-up doorways that once led off Regent Road to Huskisson Dock station, which was located on the other side and above the dock wall. The station, which was next to Huskisson Branch Dock No 1, opened in 1896 as a replacement for Sandon Dock station. *Author*

Left: A few of the LOR stanchions and floor bumpers remain at Wapping, as seen here in the dock wall in April 2006. The box steel columns, 1ft wide and 16ft high, were riveted in pairs, and their sturdy cast-iron bumpers were manufactured in Liverpool by Francis Morton & Co. The size of the concrete foundations depended on the nature of the ground, but 7ft x 6ft x 5ft 9in was usual. *Author*

Above right: Located in the heart of a densely populated area, Dingle station was unique in being the only underground station on the LOR. In 1901 a fire on a train in the station killed six people — the most serious loss of life in the railway's history. The white tiled subway and underground station still survive, although the latter is nowadays used as a garage, and a few original features remain. Note, however, the LOR monogram on the keystone, photographed in September 2006. *Author*

Right: First-class trailer car No 7 — the only survivor of the LOR's modernised fleet — at the Coventry Railway Centre on 17 June 2007. Despite suffering some damage in a shunting accident it has retained its two-tone brown livery throughout the 50 years since the line closed. *Author*

7 Change at Liverpool Exchange

In the spring of 1850 a station was opened in Liverpool's Tithebarn Street, taking its name from that thoroughfare. Designed by Sir John Hawkshaw in Italianate style, it resembled a grand country house and was used by both the ELR and the LYR. However, the LYR insisted on calling it Exchange station and duplicated ELR facilities on the site. This situation was resolved before the LYR absorbed the ELR in 1859, and the station became known officially as Liverpool Exchange.

As Liverpool's suburban development grew along the lines into the station, so too did passenger numbers, and the station became increasingly congested. In the 1880s it was rebuilt, partially reopening by 1886 and being completed in 1888, to become the main LYR terminus in Liverpool. In rebuilt form it boasted a hotel, a doubling of platforms (to 10) and four lofty iron-and-glass-gabled trainsheds.

The station developed as a terminus for long-distance services, notably to and from the Lake District and Scotland. It also served the Lancashire coast, and its location on the edge of Liverpool's business district led to an increase in commuter traffic, such that by 1913 the suburban lines to Ormskirk and Southport had been electrified. Trains from Exchange also ran to Manchester, in competition with the LNWR, until the latter absorbed the LYR in 1922, and by the 1930s the station was being used by about 600 trains per day.

The station was typical of the Victorian age, with its cavernous, smoke-filled iron trainsheds, a carriage road for horse-drawn road vehicles, a stationmaster (complete with top hat) and all the bustle of a major city terminus. Following

Below: The 10-platform Exchange station was the second-busiest on the LYR, being used by trains to the Lancashire cotton towns and to key destinations in Yorkshire. This view from 1928 shows the enquiry and booking office at the end of Platforms 4 and 5, which were used by main-line trains. Note the handbills beneath the posters. By the 1930s there were about 600 trains a day, the LMS installing mechanical platform barriers to deal with the large numbers of commuters. *LPC*

BRITISH RAILWAYS

LIVERPOOL EXCHANGE STATION

Above: Stanier 2-6-4T No 42550 waits to depart Liverpool Exchange on 5 August 1963 with the 3pm to Bolton Trinity Street. Comprising four coaches, this train called at all stations and was timed to take 1hr 9min. *D. Idle*

rebuilding the station was to remain unchanged until closure. However, bomb damage sustained in World War 2 extended to the nearby viaduct, isolating the station from the rest of the network for three months, while the unrepaired damage to the roof of some of the iron trainsheds lent it a derelict air for much of its existence postwar; this was particularly so in the 1970s, when closure was in prospect and little maintenance was undertaken.

In 1967, by which time long-distance trains were gradually being cut back, three platforms were levelled to provide space for car parking. History was made on Sunday 3 August 1968, when there arrived at the terminus an express from Glasgow that became widely recognised as the last long-distance scheduled steam-hauled train on BR.

Thereafter most remaining long-distance services were diverted to Lime Street station. Exchange station closed on 29 April 1977, when a piped lament bade farewell to the last services. A new underground line was opened shortly afterwards, allowing the electrified suburban services to continue into the centre of Liverpool, and consequently the area is still served by rail.

The main iron trainsheds were demolished soon after closure, but the stone façade of the former hotel building in Tithebarn Street was retained; located in Liverpool's commercial district, it is now used as offices. By 2008 a car park occupied much of the station site but included ruined remains of the station. Further details can be found in *Lost Lines: LMR*.

Left: A snapshot in time. Towards the end of the BR steam era — at 1.48pm on Tuesday 27 September 1966, to be precise — Stanier 'Black Five' 4-6-0 No 44816 moves empty stock out of Liverpool Exchange station. Most platforms were 200yd long and could accommodate express trains. *W. Power*

Below left: The LYR developed most of its passenger services to the north of Liverpool. 'Black Five' 4-6-0 No 44950 is seen simmering after arrival at Liverpool Exchange on 19 May 1968 with the 16.43 from Preston. The final leg of this journey, from Ormskirk, had taken just over 14 minutes, a speed of 80mph being recorded through Maghull. *J. Berry*

Above right: A two-coach DMU forming the 12.53 to Bolton accelerates away from Liverpool Exchange on 18 March 1973. This is, perhaps, an indication of the decline in passenger numbers since the steam departure to Bolton, with four coaches, 10 years earlier, although more seating was provided in a DMU coach than in one that was locomotive-hauled. *P. Hanson*

Liverpool ..	Manchester	Liverpool Central and Manchester Central via Padgate **or** Liverpool Exchange and Manchester Vic. via Daisy Hill **or** via Moses Gate **or** Liverpool Lime St. and Manchester Exchange via Eccles.

Below: Ready to depart as the 18.10 to Southport (foreground) and the 18.15 to Ormskirk, LMS-built EMUs (later Class 502) await commuters in the gathering gloom of Exchange station on 24 October 1964. *J. Clarke*

Above: The three alternative routes from Liverpool to Manchester as listed by BR in 1962.

Left: Hurrying to catch the 12.24 EMU to Southport at Liverpool Exchange in July 1970. Note the rather dilapidated train indicator, designed originally to show the sequence of the next two platform departures. The service was electrified (by means of a third rail, energised at 625V DC) by the LYR as far back as 1904. At that time almost half of all seats provided were for First-class passengers, indicating the importance of commuter traffic. *S. Lovell*

Below: A Class 502 EMU arrives at Liverpool Exchange from Ormskirk on 9 April 1971. These units were built by the LMS in the years 1939-41 and replaced the original LYR electric stock of 1904. Although Exchange was a popular station, being conveniently located for Liverpool's business district, its deliberate neglect by BR in favour of Lime Street is apparent from this view. *R. Carrell*

Above: The last services to use the station were all electric. Here a Class 502 EMU departs for Southport during the final week of operation, in April 1977. Cars have already colonised Platforms 1-3 (on the left), while the partly roofless condition of one of the four trainsheds adds to the general air of desolation. The Class 502s would all be withdrawn by 1981. *J. Gross*

Right: The side entrances to Liverpool Exchange station's parcel depot in Pall Mall remain extant, albeit in derelict condition. One is seen here in April 2006, long after the main facilities were demolished by Oldham Bros. It is interesting to note that the station frontage (which also survives) was built of stone, whereas the sides were mainly of brick. *Author*

⑧ Contraction at Liverpool Central

The Cheshire Lines Committee was established in 1865. It was the second-largest joint railway in Britain, and its Liverpool–Manchester line was one of its key routes, competing with the LNWR and LYR. The headquarters of the railway were located at Liverpool Central station, which was the last main-line station to open in Liverpool, in March 1874, and was served by the three railway companies that operated the CLC — the GCR, MR and GNR.

Liverpool Central was constructed on a restricted city-centre site. The approach to the station was also difficult, via the 1,009yd Central Tunnel, and the line from Brunswick took some time to construct, mainly because tunnelling so close to the city centre had to be undertaken without explosives. From 1892 the Mersey Railway would provide an underground station at this location.

Part of the high-level station's attractive stone façade was hidden by a covered road entrance, parcels office, advertisements and other paraphernalia abutting the main entrance. Nevertheless it occupied a commanding position on Ranelagh Street and was well placed in the centre of Liverpool. The single-span arched roof, some 65ft (19.8m) in height, was a key feature and became a familiar landmark of the city.

In 1875 the Marple curve was constructed, linking the CLC with the Midland Railway. This allowed direct running to London, and in April a night Pullman sleeper service to St Pancras was introduced. Services also ran to the Great Central main line, and even after the 1923 Grouping, which left the CLC as a separate operating entity, the LNER ran services to Marylebone, while the LMS ran to St Pancras.

The Liverpool Central–Manchester route benefited from the introduction of one of the first even-interval timetables, the 'Punctual Service' leaving Liverpool Central at 30 minutes past each hour, and in the late 19th century the 40-minute

Below: The plans for Central station were prepared by Charles Vignoles. The main building, pictured c1900, served as the headquarters of the Cheshire Lines Committee. In the foreground (left) is the parcels office, while just visible in the background is Lewis's original department store. The latter building would be destroyed during World War 2 but subsequently replaced; the station buildings would be destroyed after the war by BR. *Liverpool Record Office, Liverpool Libraries*

journey provided the fastest regular express trains in the world. Services developed, and at one time Central station was the most heavily used departure-point for passengers travelling from Liverpool to Manchester. Some faraway destinations were also once directly served by the station, including Cromer and Brighton. Even in the 1960s, in addition to suburban services, through trains still ran as far as Harwich, Hull and London.

Central station competed with both Lime Street and Exchange to provide services to Manchester, and closure proposals were perhaps inevitable under the Beeching 'axe' to remove any form of duplication. Consequently in 1966 main-line services were diverted to Lime Street. However, the station continued in use for local trains to Gateacre, on the ex-CLC line to Aintree, using just two platforms and giving Central station an air of dereliction and impending closure. The Gateacre service continued until April 1972, and even then it was indicated that closure of the line would be temporary and that the electrification and reopening as far as Gateacre were part of the new proposals. This was not to be, although electric passenger services did recommence from the low-level station as far as Hunts Cross, and today the low-level station, with its ex-MeR and new services, is as busy as ever.

After a brief period of dereliction most of the high-level station, including the fine trainshed, was

Above: A staircase from the CLC's Liverpool Central High Level station (as it was known from 1966) leads to the Mersey Railway's Low Level station below. The convenience of the interchange is apparent in this photograph taken in LNER days. The LNER owned two thirds of the CLC, the LMS the remainder. The enamel map shows Wirral railways and indicates the journey time to Hamilton Square — then, as now, 5 minutes. *BR*

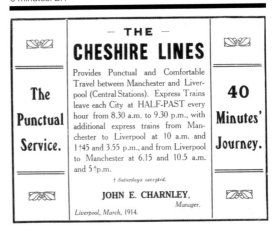

— THE —
CHESHIRE LINES

The Punctual Service.

Provides Punctual and Comfortable Travel between Manchester and Liverpool (Central Stations). Express Trains leave each City at HALF-PAST every hour from 8.30 a.m. to 9.30 p.m., with additional express trains from Manchester to Liverpool at 10 a.m. and 1†45 and 3.55 p.m., and from Liverpool to Manchester at 6.15 and 10.5 a.m. and 5†p.m.

† Saturdays excepted.

JOHN E. CHARNLEY, Manager.

Liverpool, March, 1914.

40 Minutes' Journey.

demolished by BR. In 2008 a Network Rail depot occupied much of the station site, while the bridge carrying Newington Street across the deep void once occupied by the station, also remained, together with a nearby footbridge and the erstwhile enquiry office in Bold Street.

Left: Bringing some continued GCR character to the heart of the city, Class D11/1 'Improved Director' 4-4-0 No 62662 *Prince of Wales* stands at Liverpool Central on 4 April 1953, having arrived with the 2.30pm from Manchester. The size of the turntable limited the types of locomotive that could use the terminus. *S. Creer*

Right: Stanier 2-6-4T No 42560 arrives at Liverpool Central on 5 August 1963 with the 4.51pm from Irlam. The station was reached by tunnel from Brunswick. The signalbox (right) was erected on a restricted site against the station wall. *D. Idle*

Left: From 1959 steam traction at Liverpool Central was gradually replaced by DMUs, one of which is seen beneath the station's distinctive 65ft-high arched roof on 24 October 1964, having arrived as the 9.43am from Gateacre. In 1966 a link at Allerton would allow most trains to be diverted from Central to Lime Street, but the Gateacre service would continue until 1972. *J. Clarke*

Left: A view of the main station building in the 1960s. The clock is probably not working, litter is strewn over the tracks, and a general air of impending closure pervades the scene. *D. Lawrence*

Right: Three island platforms originally provided six platform faces. By 28 October 1967, however, the once noble headquarters of the CLC presented a sad sight, with just two lines and a single DMU service remaining, the deserted platforms being occupied by parked cars. *Ian Allan Library*

Left: A DMU arriving from Gateacre still provides a busy scene at Liverpool Central in July 1970. The plan had been to withdraw the service earlier, but problems in providing a satisfactory alternative bus service led to a delay in the final closure of the station. *S. Lovel*

45

Above: On 14 April 1972, the day before closure, a DMU awaits passengers at Liverpool Central. In its last days the surviving service ran from a shortened Platform 4; most had been transferred to Lime Street several years previously. *J. Cadman*

Left: A crudely shorn-off metal girder that once provided support for the main distinctive steel-and-glass barrel-arched roof still survived at the site of Central station in April 2006. By June 2007 all remaining stubs had been removed as part of cosmetic improvement and renovation of the walls. *Author*

Below left: Newington Bridge, spanning the void created by Central station, was still extant in April 2006, as was the Heathfield Street footbridge just visible in the background. Newington Bridge has since been repainted. *Author*

Above: Liverpool Central Low Level station was closed in July 1975. The original underground station operated just below the High Level station, the walls of which can be seen at the top left in this view. The future was not quite as bleak as the picture suggests, for the derelict low-level platforms were to witness a return of trains in April 1977, as part of the Mersey underground electrification scheme. *G. Whiting*

Right: A part of the original High Level station that still survives is the former enquiry office in Bold Street, together with the adjoining left-luggage office facing onto the pedestrian thoroughfare known as Lyceum Place. This photograph, taken from Bold Street in June 2007, gives an idea of the ornate nature of the original stone-built station. *Author*

Left: Liverpool Central High Level signalbox was on a restricted site. Although the signalbox itself has long since been demolished, a few remnants of the mechanical signalling equipment could still be found in April 2006. *Author*

⑨ Liverpool Docks

In their heyday Liverpool's docks were recognised as the finest in the world, but their success was due ultimately to railway access to the quaysides. The Edge Hill–Wapping and Waterloo dock routes opened in the 1830s and '40s. Lines onto the actual quaysides took some time to develop, and for many years the horse and cart continued to be used to transport cargoes from the ships to the railway depots.

With the docks' expansion northwards the LNWR built the Edge Hill–Bootle branch and in June 1866 provided a link to Canada Dock. In January 1880 the line was further extended, to Atlantic Dock, this being renamed Alexandra Dock when passenger services began in September 1881. The LNWR passenger service to these docks ran some 7½ miles from Lime Street, via Edge Hill.

The LNWR was not the only railway to provide links to the northern docks, the LYR opening its Sandhills–North Docks line in 1855 and the North Mersey branch from Aintree in 1867. The LYR also provided passenger services to Gladstone Dock, where a station was opened in September 1914 on the North Mersey branch. Passenger and freight services were provided by LYR ships to Drogheda in Ireland; these sailed from Collingwood Docks but also called at the Prince's Landing Stage, next to the Pier Head. Although this was the closest point to Exchange station it was still some distance away, and the shipping service was not revived after World War 1.

The CLC served the south docks, opening a line to Brunswick in June 1864, but as the docks grew a new line was required to the north docks. Tunnelling such a potentially busy freight line under Liverpool would have been prohibitively costly, so a circuitous route around the city's eastern outskirts was built to provide a link to the north docks at Huskisson. Passenger services to Huskisson commenced in August 1880 but lasted just five years. From the CLC line the Midland Railway built the short Huskisson–Sandon Dock freight link and in 1885 opened the Fazakerley Junction–Alexandra Dock line.

The movement of passengers through Liverpool Docks led to the opening, with great ceremony in June 1895, of the MD&HB's Riverside station. This quayside terminus was linked to Edge Hill and was used by LNWR boat trains connecting with the ocean liners to America. Even when it was newly opened trains were infrequent, and on average only two per week used the station. In latter years, on account of weight restrictions in the docks two

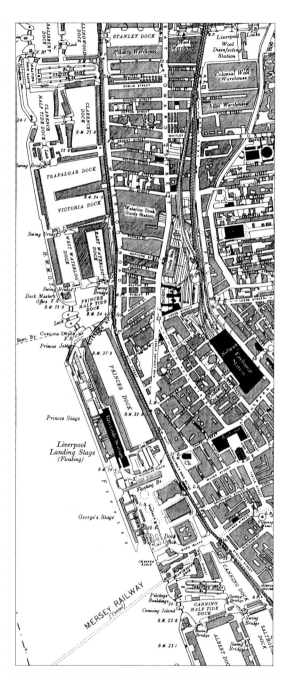

Above: Liverpool Riverside station and the adjoining dockside area in 1928. *Crown Copyright*

special tank engines were employed to work the boat trains between Edge Hill and Riverside. This short journey was slow, taking about half an hour, because in the dock area the line wound its way among other dock lines and roadways. In 1946 improvements were made that allowed almost direct access to the transatlantic liners from Riverside station, and later BR strengthened Prince's Dock Bridge, which allowed through locomotive running from London.

The MD&HB developed about 60 miles of track in the Liverpool dock area. These lines penetrated all parts and eventually linked the entire length of the dock complex. Other railway companies were allowed access to the quaysides over its lines, and in 1904 about 14 million tons of cargo passed through the docks, which extended for more than 6 miles, from Dingle to Seaforth Sands.

During World War 2 the docks and Liverpool generally constituted the most heavily bombed area outside London. By way of example, in 1941 alone the GWR lost its James Street offices, Pier Head offices and warehouse and its Lightbody Street office, warehouse and timber-stacking yard. The docks were equally heavily used throughout the war, and some 4.7 million troops passed through during the conflict, including 1.7 million through Riverside station.

By the end of the war freight using the MD&HB was reduced to about 4 million tons annually, and in 1955 only 68 ships called at Liverpool. Canada Dock station, closed by bombing in 1941, never

reopened. Passenger services to Alexandra Dock ended in 1949, and freight in 1967. The North Mersey branch closed to passengers in April 1951. Transatlantic liners also were making less frequent use of Liverpool: Riverside station slipped into decline and closed in February 1971, being demolished after a period of dereliction. Today none of the passenger stations in the dock area remains.

The 1970s saw continued economic decline, and by 1972 only about 150,000 tons of freight was being handled annually by the MD&HB. Rail working to the southern docks ceased in 1971, following which all the remaining south docks closed to traditional commercial traffic. Rail access to the north docks ended in September 1973.

After a long decline the remaining north docks saw a revival. By 1984 rail-borne freight had returned to the north docks, Gladstone, Alexandra and Seaforth being rail-served. While the modern docks thrive, many fascinating buildings associated with the docks remain, and numerous railway tracks and other transport relics can still be found throughout the dock area.

Below: MD&HB 0-6-0 diesel shunter No 32 at Prince's Half-Tide dock, with a train shunting under the LOR. Half-Tide indicated that the dock gates could be opened at any time on the top half of the tide. The port had grown to become one of the mightiest in the world, and it is clear that the docks were booming when this view was recorded on 20 December 1947. Prince's Half-Tide Dock would close in 1981. *S. Bale*

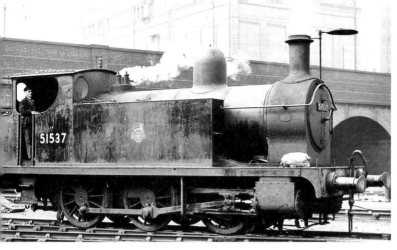

Left: Canada Dock on 11 April 1959, with 0-6-0T No 51537. The last survivor of its class, this ex-LYR locomotive, designed by Aspinall for dock work, would be scrapped in 1961. Canada Dock was involved with much of the North American timber trade, hence its name. Modernised in the 1960s, it remains open, although direct rail connections are no more. *R. C. Riley*

Left: Trains pass on the LOR in the early 1950s, with the Gladstone Dock complex, at the north end of the dock estate, in the background. Opened in 1913 and named after a chairman of the MD&HB (rather than the Victorian Prime Minister), Gladstone Dock was enlarged between 1922 and 1927 to accommodate the largest transatlantic liners. The docks remain open in modified form.
Ian Allan Library

Below left: An early-1950s view of Herculaneum Dock and, at the top left, the LOR's old Herculaneum terminus, which was used until the line was extended to Dingle in 1896. The LOR crossed over CLC tracks seen in the lower foreground. The dock took its name from the nearby Herculaneum pottery works, which specialised in marine pottery. The dock closed in 1972.
Ian Allan Library

Above right: Seen near Liverpool Pier Head while *en route* from Park Lane to the docks on 5 November 1960, ex-LYR 0-4-0ST No 51206 passes the Cunard building, with the ventilation shaft and Mersey Tunnel offices in the background. Affectionately known as 'Pugs', these short-wheelbase locomotives, built between 1891 and 1910, were designed specifically for the sharp curves of the dock lines. The last examples survived until 1962. *L. Sandler*

Right: 'Pug' No 51206 about to enter Liverpool Docks after running light from Bank Hall to Park Lane goods depot on 5 November 1960. The LOR once ran above the two tracks seen here, and the smoke-deflecting cowl over the locomotive's chimney was aimed at preventing smoke from belching with great force onto the LOR structure, although in this it was not entirely effective. All the buildings in this view have since been demolished. *L. Sandler*

Left: Crossing the swing bridge at Prince's Half-Tide Dock, ex-LNWR 0-8-0 No 49082 propels empty boat-train stock, comprising six coaches, restaurant and kitchen cars, into Riverside station in the early 1950s. Note the double signal arm; the top arm with double spectacles was to regulate the movement of shipping. *R. Hewitt*

Left: Pictured inside Riverside station on 13 June 1964, ex-LMS 'Jinty' 0-6-0T No 47486 stands at the head of a special train organised by the Liverpool University Public Transport Society for a tour of the 'Liverpool Suburban' area. Unique in being owned by the MD&HB, Riverside station had three platforms, each almost 800ft long, and during World War 2 the station was used by no fewer than 4,648 troop trains, between them conveying nearly 1¾ million servicemen. *I. Holt*

Left: The LUPTS special of 13 June 1964 also visited Alexandra Dock. Still extant in the background is the trainshed of the LNWR passenger station, opened in 1881 and closed in 1948. Although the line closed in 1973, rail-borne freight has since returned to this general location, and the dock remains open, but the old passenger station has now been demolished. *I. Holt*

Above: The 13.55 Liverpool Central–Gateacre DMU train passes Herculaneum Dock on 20 February 1968. By this time the LOR steel trellis bridge had been dismantled, and freight to the dock itself was limited. After a period of closure the ex-CLC passenger line reopened, but all the dock sidings are long gone, and the area seen here on the right has been redeveloped. *C. Gifford*

Right: Some 200 passengers took part in a tour of the docks, on 11 August 1973, as a prelude to closure of the railway at the end of the month. Six open wagons and two brake vans were hauled by the last two MD&HB 0-6-0 diesel shunters (Nos 41 and 42) that were built by Hudswell Clarke in 1962. The train is seen here at Canada branch dock No 3. *G. Hounsell*

Left: An 0-4-0 diesel shunter on display at Atlantic Avenue, Bootle, in April 2006. Small diesel locomotives were to be found within industrial complexes and were used to shunt wagons around. Locomotives had been allowed to replace horses in the dock area from 1895. *Author*

Below left: Riverside station was built to enable the port of Liverpool to compete with Southampton and for many years was used by passengers to and from America. It was demolished in the 1980s, but in April 2006 tracks were still to be found in the cobbles on the station approach. Waterloo warehouse, dating from 1868, can be seen in the far distance; originally used to store corn, it is now in residential use. The area has seen further new development since this photograph was taken. *Author*

Above: Part of a bridge abutment remained on the ex-LYR high-level coal branch in July 2007. The original bridge (beneath which the LOR once dipped on the other side of the dock wall, at Bramley Moore) could be hauled up by chains, to allow high loads to use the Dock Road. The branch opened in 1856, allowing coal wagons to discharge their loads directly into ships' bunkers, and such was the demand for Lancashire coal that in 1882 night-time working commenced. The branch remained in use until 1966. *Author*

Left: The GWR offices and warehouse at Manchester Basin depot were designed to receive barge cargoes from Morpeth Docks at Birkenhead for delivery in Liverpool. Freight was once also received via the goods ferry or 'luggage boats', as they were called locally. The GWR signs seen in this photograph (taken in July 2000) of the revitalised dock area appear to have been added later. *Author*

10 Subterranean steam

Plans for a double-deck steam ferry, conveying railway stock across the Mersey, were abandoned when the Mersey Railway was built to connect Liverpool with Birkenhead by means of a tunnel under the river. Opened by the Prince of Wales in February 1886, this was a remarkable engineering work, being one of the longest underwater railways at that time, the tunnel having been excavated by hand and by means of explosives.

It was recognised from the outset that steam power would not be ideal, but the gradients from deep under the Mersey made cable haulage impractical, and an atmospheric system was proposed. However, such systems were not reliable, and even Brunel's atmospheric line in Devon was one of his few failures. As a consequence the longest underwater railway at the time was forced to rely on steam. Its fleet included a class of nine powerful locomotives with the biggest cylinders ever provided at that time. Services began operating in February 1886, running some 4 miles underground from Green Lane, Birkenhead, to James Street, Liverpool. An extension to Rock Ferry opened in 1891, and another to Liverpool Central the following year.

The gradient from 39ft below Ordnance datum under the Mersey to James Street station included a section of 1 in 27 (and is now the steepest passenger gradient remaining on Britain's national rail network). Although huge steam-operated ventilation fans were used, and the locomotives equipped with condensing apparatus, the frequency of trains running in opposite directions through the double-track tunnels still resulted in the air in the underground stations becoming foul and sulphurous as the trains slogged up the exceptionally steep gradients from deep under the river.

So many preferred the fresh air of the Mersey ferries that, following the opening of the railway, they continued to convey a great number of passengers, while the costs of ventilation and drainage added to the railway's financial problems. The situation became so bad that the heavy capital expenditure of electrification, with a 650V DC fourth-rail system, was agreed, the work being undertaken by Westinghouse. The line thus became the first underwater electrified railway, the last steam-worked subterranean passenger train running on 3 May 1903. The line's murky stations were cleaned, and, although the new stock was somewhat basic, with no heating (or upholstery in Third class), passenger numbers increased, and the line was saved.

The locomotives were sold off by public auction, and being relatively youthful, many were acquired for further use. Three found a home in South Wales and later passed to part of the GWR. Four went to Australia, where some survived until the 1950s (and one — No 1 *The Major* — until the 1960s). Two were acquired by Shipley Collieries, including No 5 *Cecil Raikes*, which remained in service for more than 50 years, until 1954. Nos 1 and 5 are both still extant.

The line surrendered its independence in 1948 but is certainly not lost; indeed, it is one of the most intensively used underground lines outside London.

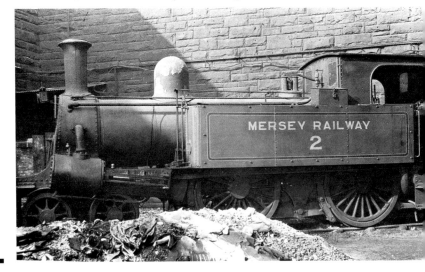

Right: The Mersey Railway's steam-operated extraction fans proved inadequate for clearing the sulphurous smoke and steam that belched from locomotives using the underwater tunnel. Seen at Birkenhead Central station is the railway's last steam locomotive, an ex-Metropolitan Railway 4-4-0T, which continued to be used for maintenance work following the introduction of electric traction and as such was the last steam locomotive to operate regularly in the Mersey Tunnel. *Real Photos*

Surviving relics from the steam era include the lofty tower at Hamilton Square, which once housed the water tanks for the huge hydraulically powered passenger lift down to the station. A similar tower at James Street has been demolished. The steam-operated Shore Road pumping station at Birkenhead, built in 1885 to clear water from the railway tunnel, is still in existence and open to the public. A similarly distinctive building is to be found in Liverpool near James Street.

Left: An ex-MeR 0-6-4T, formerly No 5 *Cecil Raikes*, seen as NCB No 42 during its time at Shipley Collieries. This was one of nine powerful 67-ton locomotives built for the underground railway in 1886 by Beyer Peacock with, at that time, the largest cylinders in the country. Used by the NCB until 1954, it would subsequently be presented to the British Transport Commission for preservation, returning to Liverpool in 1965. *Ian Allan Library*

Right: Now preserved, and with ex-LOR First-class coach No 7 for company, ex-MeR 0-6-4T No 5 *Cecil Raikes* is seen at Steamport on 17 September 1981. Note that the locomotive retained its condensing apparatus, even though this had not been required during the last 50 years of its working life. *B. Morrison*

Left: Another view of *Cecil Raikes* at Steamport, this time being shunted by 0-4-0T *Efficient* on 14 June 1987. Although powerful, the MeR 0-6-4Ts had to work hard with their 150-ton trains on the gradients, as geological difficulties resulted in some sections' being as steep as 1 in 27, rather than the planned maximum of 1 in 30. This example could still be found in Liverpool in 2007, while another survives in Australia. The underground line itself is, of course, not lost and remains very busy. *T. Heavyside*

11 Seacombe Crossing

The growth of Birkenhead and surrounding areas led to the development of a suburban rail network on the Wirral peninsula, notably by the Wirral Railway. This was a small but dynamic company that had hoped to run its trains through the Mersey Tunnel to Liverpool, but the Mersey Railway would not allow this. The narrowest section of the River Mersey between Wirral and Liverpool was at Seacombe, and the WiR sought to capitalise on this by building a branch to Seacombe with an adjoining ferry link to Liverpool.

The 3-mile branch to Seacombe, with one intermediate station, involved extensive cutting through sandstone and was the last line opened by the WiR, in June 1895. Wirral Railway services ran from Seacombe (which station was renamed Seacombe & Egremont in 1901) to West Kirby and to New Brighton, but the latter destination could not compete with the more direct trams. 'The Dodger' (as the service was known), which ran mainly for the benefit of summer trippers, was withdrawn in 1911, and that part of the Bidston triangle which allowed through running to New Brighton was lifted during World War 1. The GCR continued to operate longer-distance services from Seacombe to Chester and Wrexham. After the war the number of passengers using the Seacombe ferry exceeded 20 million annually, and the double-track branch, with frequent services to West Kirby and good ferry connections to Liverpool, was well used.

A new ferry terminal building was opened at Seacombe in 1933. The station adjoined this, but the contrast between the substantial stone and brick ferry terminal, with its grand clock tower, and the small, mainly wooden passenger station, could not have been greater.

Decline began with the opening of the Mersey Queensway Tunnel in 1934. This resulted in an almost immediate reduction, by about 2 million annually, in the number of passengers using the ferry and had a knock-on effect on passenger usage of the branch line. In order to counter the road tunnel the LMS extended its Wirral electrification but ominously decided not to electrify the Seacombe branch. Consequently through services to West Kirby ceased in 1938 with the introduction of the electric service. However, the Seacombe–Wrexham trains, fondly nicknamed 'Wrexham rattlers', continued to be run by the LNER.

Seacombe & Egremont station reverted to plain 'Seacombe' in 1953, and BR also replaced the wooden island platform with a more substantial concrete affair. Nevertheless, the station retained a somewhat run-down appearance, and the line closed to passengers in January 1960, when services from Wrexham were diverted to New Brighton. The surviving freight ceased in 1963.

After closure almost all of the trackbed was used as the basis for an approach road to the Mersey Kingsway Tunnel, which opened in 1971. This resulted in the withdrawal of the New Brighton ferry, and the Seacombe ferry building also fell into disrepair. Today little remains of the railway, although the impressive ferry terminal at Seacombe has been restored, and Seacombe retains its Mersey ferry service. A frequent train service still serves New Brighton, but in 2008 trains from Wrexham terminated at Bidston.

Above: Crest of the Wirral Railway. Maps showing the Seacombe branch appear on pages 10, 67 and 73.

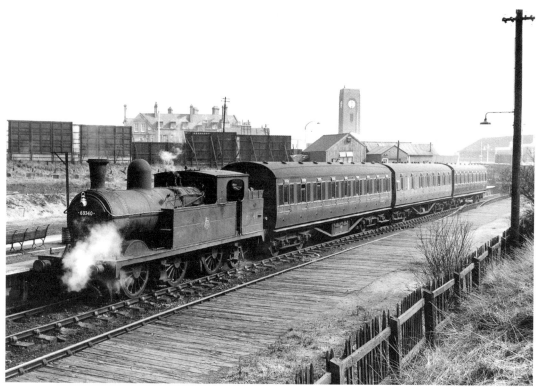

Left: GCR outpost. Class C13 No 67435, an ex-GCR 4-4-2T, departs Seacombe with a train for Wrexham on 14 March 1952. LMS electrification in the 1930s left the LNER-operated Seacombe branch and the ex-GCR link to Wrexham among the Wirral's few non-electrified lines. The Seacombe branch, the last line constructed in the area by the Wirral Railway, would be one of the early closures. *W. Garth*

Below left: Class N5 0-6-2T No 69340, one of 129 locomotives built between 1891 and 1901, departs Seacombe with a train for Wrexham on 31 March 1956. Only the single island platform was used by passengers at this time, the wooden platform in the foreground being out of regular use. The clock tower in the background is part of the Seacombe ferry terminal. *S. Creer*

Above: Ivatt 2-6-2T No 41231 arrives at Seacombe on 16 May 1959 with the 11.25am from Wrexham. On the right, marked 'SEACOMBE STATION CABIN', can be seen the distinctive WiR signalbox, with its overhanging roof. In BR days the branch was not seen as a key link across the Mersey and became increasingly marginalised before closure in 1960. *M. Walshaw*

Below: End of the line. No 41231 runs round its train on 16 May 1959. The basic nature of the station is apparent. Receipts from the branch never allowed renewal of the somewhat meagre passenger terminus, although a concrete platform was provided, gas lighting was replaced by electric, and some track re-ballasting was undertaken. *M. Walshaw*

Left: BR Standard Class 3 2-6-2T No 82020, one of 45 such locomotives built between 1952 and 1955, approaches the sturdy Seacombe home signal on 16 May 1959, ready to work the 12.45pm passenger train to Wrexham. The deep sandstone cutting seen here is now occupied by a dual-carriageway road leading to the Kingsway Tunnel under the Mersey. *M. Walshaw*

Below: No 82020 departs Seacombe with the 12.45pm to Wrexham on 16 May 1959. Day-trippers, in particular Liverpudlians heading for North Wales, provided important additional revenue for the branch, while even until closure commuters could still be seen using the service on their way to the ferry for Liverpool. *M. Walshaw*

Above: Ivatt 2-6-2T No 41231 arrives at the only intermediate station on the branch, at Liscard & Poulton, with the 1.35pm from Seacombe on 16 May 1959. The attractive station had a gas-lit island platform and a booking office at street level. Nowadays a busy road runs right through this location, the only evidence of the railway being the access to the station yard cut through the sandstone. *M. Walshaw*

Left: By the 1920s the Seacombe ferry was carrying millions of passengers a year, and in 1933 the current ferry terminal replaced a smaller building. However, the opening of the Queensway Tunnel had a detrimental effect on passengers and goods using the ferry, and the Seacombe luggage boats ceased in 1947. The Kingsway Tunnel had a similar effect in reducing passengers, but the ferry continued. Part of the terminal is seen here in September 2006. *Author*

Below: All that remains of the railway at Seacombe is the wall of an overbridge (seen here in September 2006), and the location is today a far cry from the freight yard and bustling interchange that was once provided by the railway and trams. *Author*

12 GWR to Woodside

The Chester–Birkenhead line opened in September 1840, and a branch was extended to Monks Ferry in 1844. There was rapid development at Birkenhead, and in 1860 the line became the Birkenhead Railway with joint GWR/LNWR ownership. In March 1878 a steeply graded 565yd tunnel link opened to the substantial new terminal station at Birkenhead Woodside. Monks Ferry closed to passengers when Woodside opened, but the station remained in use for goods until 1961.

Woodside was a distinctive and imposing station. The main entrance had a high-vaulted wooden roof, enormous fireplaces and a stylishness that lent it an almost cathedral-like air. The five platforms and seven tracks were spanned by two trainsheds with barrel-vaulted iron-and-glass roofs. There was intricate brickwork, carved stonework and a huge clock, while gothic features were to be found throughout the structure.

The main station entrance was intended to lead, via a covered way, to the Mersey ferry terminal but in fact was never used as it led to the ferry workshops, which were never re-sited. Consequently a 'temporary' structure was used as the main entrance throughout the lifetime of the station, the planned main entrance serving only as a parcels office. This temporary entrance, in addition to being close to the ferry, also provided a more convenient interchange for nearby trams and buses serving the Birkenhead area.

The GWR promoted its route to Birkenhead, and the first steam-heated corridor train ran from Woodside to Paddington in March 1892, and for a short time the GWR ran through carriages under the River Mersey to Liverpool Central Low Level station, where it opened its own parcels office. A similar experiment was undertaken with buses that used the Mersey ferries to Liverpool. These links were not a great success, and Woodside station, on the Birkenhead bank of the River Mersey, provided the GWR with its grand access to Liverpool, via the ferries, for the rest of its existence.

For many years the station was well used, with, at its peak, more than 25 departures to London on each weekday. The aftermath of World War 2 saw the closure of Birkenhead Town station by the LMS and GWR in 1945, but Woodside's decline, including decay of the fabric of the station itself under BR, took many years. Trains to Margate ceased running in 1959, and those to Bournemouth in 1961, although summer excursion trains to North Wales were still running at that time.

Closure was first considered in 1962 and was confirmed in 1965. Express trains continued to run

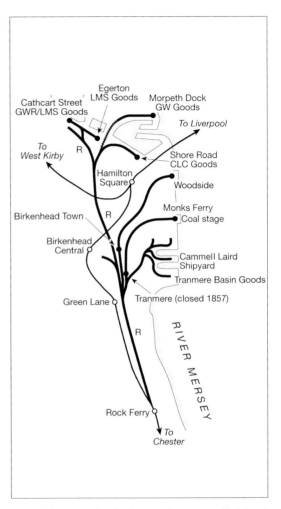

to Paddington, including a sleeper until March 1967. Although a fight was mounted against closure, this was effected on 4 November 1967, when the station closed its gates for the last time.

Although Woodside station is no longer in existence, having been demolished soon after closure, some of the retaining walls, with their ornate carved-stone copings, are still extant, while the equally handsome gates have been preserved. The Woodside ferry still operates; its terminal building, dating from 1862, survives and is now a listed building, while the line from Rock Ferry to the nearby Hamilton Square station is still open. A huge model of Woodside station is to be found in Wirral Museum, while further details of the station itself appear in *Lost Lines: LMR*.

Right: Stanier 2-6-4T No 42441 departs Birkenhead Woodside in 1963. Note the height of the station's arched glazed trainsheds. The concrete lamp standards had replaced more elegant iron gas lamps. *Ian Allan Library*

Below: BR Standard Class 4 2-6-0 No 76047 at Birkenhead Woodside, on 30 May 1966, awaiting departure with the 11.45am to Paddington. The station had a useful cross-country service to London, and until the 1950s through trains also ran to such faraway destinations as Cardiff, Dover, Plymouth and Poole.
This was the view towards the tunnel mouth, which could still be found in 2007, while the road bridge in front of it also survives. *N. Matthews*

Left: Birkenhead Woodside on 21 October 1966, with BR Standard Class 5 4-6-0 No 73160 ready to depart with the 14.45 stopping train to Wrexham; on the left is Fairburn 2-6-4T No 42086 at the head of some empty stock. Although Woodside was a relatively large terminus the third line required for locomotives to run around their trains, combined with the presence of a roadway between Platforms 1 and 2, meant that only five platforms were provided. *M. Dunnett*

Left: Another view of BR Standard Class 5 4-6-0 No 73160 waiting to depart with the 14.45 to Wrexham on 21 October 1966; note the poor condition of the platform surface. Although Woodside station is no more, local trains still run from Birkenhead. *M. Dunnett*

Right: Passing the extensive sidings that once existed to the south of Woodside Tunnel, Stanier 2-6-4T No 42613 climbs away from Birkenhead on Sunday 29 May 1966 with the 12.25 through carriages for Paddington. Almost all the lines seen here have since been lost. *B. Taylor*

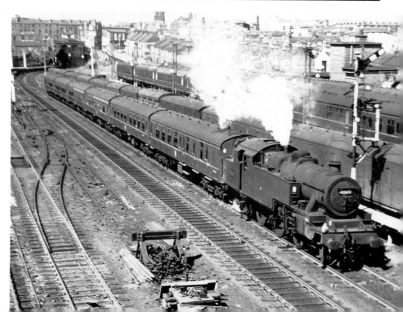

Right: To mark the end of long-distance trains to/from Woodside the Stephenson Locomotive Society organised a special to Chester. Selected for the trip was Standard Class 9F 2-10-0 No 92234, seen backing into the terminus on 5 March 1967. In the foreground is the station pilot, Stanier two-cylinder 2-6-4T No 42616. *M. Dunnett*

Right: A very well-turned-out No 92234 at Woodside, ready to work the SLS special to Chester on 5 March 1967. The '8H' shed code on the smokebox door denotes allocation to Birkenhead shed. The locomotive would be withdrawn in November 1967, after less than 10 years' service. *M. Dunnett*

Below: Also marking the end of long-distance services to Woodside were two steam-hauled specials from Birmingham. Having taken its train to Birkenhead, preserved ex-WR 'Castle' 4-6-0 No 7029 *Clun Castle* is seen on shed at Chester on 4 March 1967. *J. Alsop*

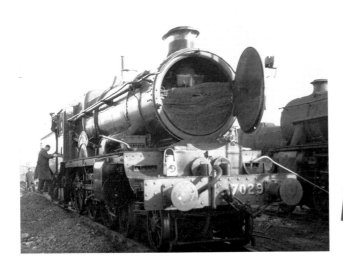

G.W.R.

LIVERPOOL

Landing Stage

Left: A quiet Woodside station in August 1967, at which date DMU services were still running to/from Chester and Helsby. In November of that year Woodside became the first major Merseyside terminus to close. No attempt was made to save the structure, which was demolished in 1969. In its prime the station had issued well over 400,000 tickets a year and employed almost 80 staff, among them the father of Wilfred Owen, the World War 1 poet. *Author*

Below left: A few of the elegantly carved capping stones at Woodside remain; this photograph, which gives a hint of the station's elegance, was taken in September 2007, some 40 years after the author first visited the site. Fortunately the nearby station at Hamilton Square and the Woodside ferry terminal still survive. *Author*

Bottom left: The partially blocked Chester Street Tunnel entrance at Woodside in April 2006. A signal gantry was once located in front of the 565yd tunnel, which was on a 1-in-93 gradient. Spoil from the tunnel helped to fill the nearby Tranmere Pool and permitted the development of Mollington Street engine sheds on the reclaimed land. Much of the station site is currently used as a bus depot. *Author*

Below: The original iron gates from Woodside station survived and, albeit rather more heavily gilded, can still be found on the Wirral peninsula, at Gayton. This photograph was taken in September 2006.
The impressive size and elegant appearance of the gates give an idea of the scale and ornateness of the station. *Author*

13 Birkenhead Docks

The development of docks at Birkenhead was perceived as a threat to Liverpool, and land was purchased by Liverpool Corporation with the aim of thwarting growth at Birkenhead. However, there was disquiet that public money was being spent in this way, and the Birkenhead land was sold off, in small lots, including to William Laird. The new owners got together to build a dock, and in 1847 the Morpeth and Egerton docks were opened.

The docks at Birkenhead were served from the outset by the Chester & Birkenhead Railway. This became the Birkenhead Railway, which in 1860 was vested in the GWR and LNWR. In 1857, meanwhile, the Liverpool and Birkenhead docks were consolidated into one estate under the MD&HB. Although there was still some concern that Birkenhead could be held back by Liverpool interests, in 1860 water was allowed to fill the 110 acres of the Great Float, a huge new dock which had been formed by using Egerton Dock as an entrance.

Birkenhead's docks were a success, and by the early 1870s a considerable railway network had developed to serve the quaysides. The Birkenhead Railway (LNWR and GWR), the WiR, CLC and GCR all served the dock complex, and all had their own goods stations in the area.

Coal was particularly important in the early years, being used by steamships. By 1885 the number of coal trains arriving at Birkenhead each week from South Wales had reached a peak of about 170, but with the building of new docks in South Wales this traffic had ceased by 1895.

Locomotives from the Vulcan Foundry and Beyer Peacock were exported from Birkenhead. By the mid-1920s about 50 miles of MD&HB railway line had been laid at Birkenhead Docks, while on the southern approaches to Birkenhead were to be found about 50 acres of railway yards and sidings.

The GWR attached great importance to handling Liverpool's freight traffic from Birkenhead, much of which was conveyed across the Mersey on goods ferries. Morpeth Dock was served by the GWR, which rebuilt its goods station in 1925, in early anticipation of using the first Mersey road tunnel.

The names given by the GWR to many of its freight trains from Birkenhead Docks, including the 'Farmer's Boy' and the 'Flying Skipper', give an idea of the diversity of freight being carried.

Until the outbreak of World War 2 the docks and railways were used extensively, including by local flour milling industries. During World War 2 they were equally busy, and, in a reversal of trade, for a time American Baldwin locomotives were imported to help with the war effort. The level of traffic fell after World War 2, but new equipment at Bidston Dock in the early 1950s prompted an increase in iron-ore traffic. Also important was the cattle trade from Ireland. At first this involved the import of live cattle, but improvements in refrigeration later allowed meat to be conveyed in refrigerated form.

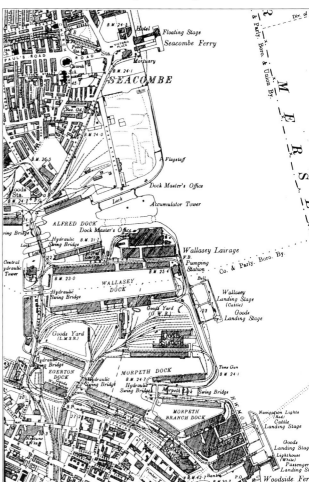

Right: The estuarine part of Birkenhead Docks, between Seacombe and Woodside stations, in 1928. *Crown Copyright*

Left: Being beckoned to cross the Egerton hydraulic bascule bridge, the 09.15 local goods leaves Morpeth Dock at Birkenhead in August 1967. The bridge, which had a 4mph speed limit, remains, but the railway tracks at this particular dockland location have gone. *I. Krause*

Right: Birkenhead Docks in March 1966, with a Crosti-boilered Class 9F 2-10-0 waiting for the Canning Street North signalman to open the crossing gates. The crossing gates, footbridge and signalbox at this location all still survived in 2008, albeit in a derelict condition. *M. Baker*

Left: Diesel shunters Nos D2238 and D2199 head towards the bascule bridge between Alfred Dock and the East Float, on Four Bridges Road, with vans for Wallasey Dock on 19 April 1968. A copy of a Florentine building, the hydraulic tower of 1863 had been damaged during World War 2 and crudely restored. Rusting lines to its entrance remained in 2007. *C. Gifford*

Until the 1950s about 200 cattle wagons were required daily for the dock cattle trains.

A decline in general rail-borne freight continued. Birkenhead did not deal with containers, and by the 1970s some parts of the dock estate were derelict. Morpeth Dock goods station was the last to close, in 1972. The ore trains ceased running in April 1980. An occasional dock freight train, particularly for grain, continued to run until the late 1980s, and the remaining freight line to Birkenhead Docks was last used in May 1993.

Surviving remnants include a number of bascule bridges, as well as the ex-CLC Shore Road and ex-LNWR Egerton warehouses. Wallasey and Bidston docks have been filled in, and Morpeth and Egerton docks have been 'environmentally improved' as water features, but the East and West Floats are still used. Although there has been much redevelopment, many interesting railway features and disused sidings were still to be found in 2008, notably the disused and heavily overgrown ex-BJR freight lines into the docks.

Right: Birkenhead Docks on 31 July 1980, with Class 47 No 47 202 on an up coal train. In the 1980s rail-borne freight declined, and the area seen here would soon become disused and overgrown, although the main Birkenhead Docks remain open.
T. Thompson

Below: Duke Street Dock at Birkenhead on Sunday 20 January 1985. Class 40 No 40 012 is seen on standby for engineering works on the Bidston line, about one mile west of the docks; the train could not move from here because sister locomotive No 40 194 had come off the rails at Bidston East Junction. Some overgrown tracks remained here in 2008, together with one of the distinctive dockside cranes.
D. Hunt

Left: Birkenhead Docks on 3 May 1985, with Class 25 No 25 035 approaching Canning Street North signalbox. The cargo is grain, which was once a very important source of rail-borne freight at Birkenhead Docks. The ship on the right is the Isle of Man Steam Packet's *Ben my Chree*, which ceased to sail from Merseyside that year. The tracks seen here still survived in 2007 but were disused and heavily overgrown. *R. Cragg*

Below left: Duke Street Bridge on 4 February 1987, with MD&HB tracks still in place. The mammoth bascule bridge divided the East and West Floats and had replaced an earlier bridge in 1931. The Great Float was so named because it kept boats afloat at all stages of the tide. There was once a road toll and a 4mph speed restriction for freight trains over this bridge. This view remained almost unchanged in 2008, apart from the removal of the rail lines in the road. *R. Ruffell*

Above right: The 'Birkenhead Docker No 2' — the 13th special organised by the Wirral Railway Circle and hauled by *Efficient*, a preserved Barclay 0-4-0ST dating from 1918 — at the Bidston yard of Rea Ltd on 10 July 1971. The rail-served berths and massive cranes at Bidston Dock handled imported iron ore, which until 1980 was conveyed thence by rail to the steelworks at Shotton. *Ian Allan Library*

Right: The 'Birkenhead Docker No 3', another railway enthusiasts' special train arranged by the Wirral Railway Circle for a tour of dock lines, this time on 1 July 1972. The double-headed train of brake vans and open wagons was photographed at Morpeth Dock, with the Liverpool skyline as a backdrop. *R. Stewart*

Above left: The footbridge adjoining the level crossing and Canning Street North signalbox, photographed in September 2006, at which time track remained *in situ*, as did the railway facilities in derelict condition. The ex-BJR line ended a few yards on from this point, that beyond being the property of the MD&HB. *Author*

Above: Another of bascule design, Egerton Bridge was built for the MD&HB in 1932 by Sir William Arrol & Co of Glasgow and has been preserved as part of the heritage of the area. This photograph was taken in April 2006. On the right can be seen Egerton Dock goods depot, opened in 1873 by the LNWR and used nowadays as offices. *Author*

Centre left: A disused wagon turntable near the East Float, seen in September 2006. Turntables such as this were often used as an alternative to points. The nearby Duke Street Bridge is still used by road traffic. Birkenhead Docks too remain open but in 2007 were not served by rail, and throughout the dock estate the once-extensive network of rail lines and sidings is gradually being swept away by new development. *Author's collection*

Left: Although not strictly part of the Birkenhead Dock complex, the Cammell Laird shipyard was an integral feature of Birkenhead's waterfront and had its own network of rail sidings. Here, on 28 May 1982, a diesel shunting locomotive belonging to the shipyard is being prepared for removal to the Steamport centre at Southport. *B. Allen*

Parkgate, on the western shore of the Wirral peninsula, was a packet port for Dublin before this part of the Dee Estuary silted up in the 1820s. It also became a bathing and fishing resort, for a time the most fashionable in the north. Also affected by the silting-up of the Dee were the coal mines at nearby Neston, and this prompted the Birkenhead Railway, which had been taken over jointly by the GWR and LNWR, to construct a 4½-mile line from Hooton to Parkgate, which opened in October 1866.

An earlier, more ambitious plan to cross the Dee estuary on an embankment from Parkgate to Flint, on the North Wales coast, which would have reclaimed some 8,000 acres of land, had received little backing. Consequently in April 1886 a new through station was opened at Parkgate, and the line was extended to run along the Wirral coast to a new Joint station adjoining the Wirral Railway's existing station at West Kirby. The line was single, with passing loops at most stations, but with capacity to be doubled in the future should traffic ever warrant it. Although usage was never heavy enough to justify more than a single line, by 1875 colliery sidings were in operation at Neston.

As residential development on the Wirral peninsula grew, commuting was encouraged by the railway, and additional intermediate stations were opened, at Kirby Park (in 1894) and Caldy (1909). Indeed, such was the spread of housing at this time that there were sufficient First-class passengers for Heswall to have its own club carriage, which was added to peak-hour trains in the years leading up to World War 1. The line was also used at weekends by day-trippers to West Kirby, Parkgate and Thurstaston. On occasions special excursion trains were also run, notably for the Wirral Hunt Steeplechase.

After the line was taken over by the LMS and GWR in 1923, a through New Brighton–Euston coach was introduced on this route (and later added to Woodside services), which practice continued until World War 2. However, the existence of more direct bus services to Birkenhead, coupled with the fact that some of the stations were a considerable distance from the villages they served, resulted in a decline in patronage postwar, and by the 1950s most passenger services were worked by a single-coach motor train. Further economies were made in February 1954 by closing Caldy and Thurstaston stations, while Kirby Park closed in July, although schools traffic continued to use this station for a further two years. However, the closure of intermediate stations was not enough to save the

line, and passenger services between West Kirby and Hooton passenger were withdrawn in September 1956. The coal pits at Neston had closed by 1927, but the occasional excursion and general freight on the line continued until May 1962. The track was lifted in 1964, although Thurstaston coal yard, latterly served by road, survived until 1976.

Following a period of dereliction, the majority of the trackbed between Hooton and West Kirby reopened in 1973 as the basis of the 12-mile Wirral Way, one of the first country parks in England. There remains much of railway interest, including various station buildings, platforms and bridges. The one-time stationmaster's house at Parkgate survives, as does that at Heswall, while at Hadlow Road the entire passenger station has been preserved.

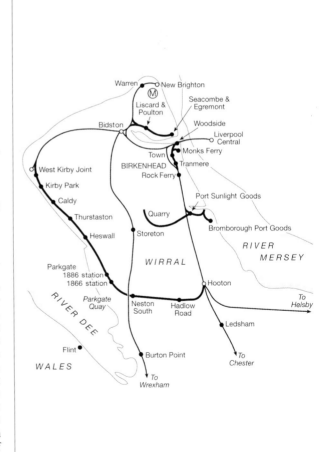

Table 112a

HOOTON and WEST KIRBY

Miles		Week Days only			
—	Hooton.............. dep				
1½	Hadlow Road.........				
3¼	Neston South........				
4½	Parkgate............				
7	Heswall.............				
12	West Kirby.......... arr				

Miles		Week Days only			
—	West Kirby.......... dep				
5	Heswall.............				
7½	Parkgate............				
8½	Neston South........				
10½	Hadlow Road.........				
12	Hooton.............. arr				

A Third class only
B From Birkenhead (Table 113)
E Except Saturdays
F To Birkenhead (Table 113)
F Arr 3 minutes earlier
H To Rock Ferry (Table 113)
S Saturdays only
T Third class only except on Saturdays
U From Birkenhead on Saturdays (Table 113)
V To Birkenhead on Saturdays (Table 113)

Left: The view north at the ex-BJR West Kirby Joint station in the 1950s, with ex-GWR '51xx' 2-6-2T No 4126 standing at the platform after heading a train from Hooton. Here locomotives ran around from one end of the train to the other and were filled with water, although the introduction of motor trains obviated the need for such shunting arrangements. *D. Lawrence*

Below left: Hooton–West Kirby timetable, July 1955.

Bottom left: Another view of West Kirby Joint in the 1950s, with the signalbox in the background and a Stanier Class 3 2-6-2T on a passenger train. The 'Joint' suffix was added to distinguish it from the nearby WiR station. Complaints that the two were not linked once the LMS took over led to the introduction of some through workings. *D. Lawrence*

Top right: The main station buildings at Thurstaston — an attractive coastal location where Lever Bros had bought land to provide a holiday camp for its Port Sunlight employees — were located on the landward platform. This view, featuring the station building and LNWR-designed signalbox, was recorded from a train in the 1950s, after the platform canopy had been removed. The station was closed as an economy measure in 1954. *D. Lawrence*

Above right: Thurstaston station on 30 April 1952, with a goods train waiting for the down local to West Kirby to clear the single line. Ex-GWR '57xx' 0-6-0PT No 3776 is in charge. In February 1957 this would be the scene of a head-on collision between a goods from West Kirby and a stationary locomotive at the head of another goods train; both locomotives were damaged, and four wagons derailed, but there were no serious injuries. *R. Hewitt*

Right: The stylish station building at Parkgate, dating from 1886, seen from a departing train in the 1950s. The mainly wooden buildings were of similar design on both sides of the track, while the platforms were linked by a gas-lit subway. The original station at Parkgate, built as a terminus in 1866 but rendered obsolete when the line was extended to West Kirby, was developed as a goods facility. *D. Lawrence*

Left: A Railway Correspondence & Travel Society special headed by an Ivatt Class 2 2-6-0 calls at Thurstaston after closure of the line to regular passenger services in September 1956. Amongst other specials to use the line were munitions trains during World War 2, the RAF making use of the platform at West Kirby Joint station after its closure to regular passengers, while 1957 witnessed a Royal Train working. The last goods train would travel over the line in May 1962, the track being lifted in 1964 following a period of dereliction. *D. Lawrence*

Below: Intervention by the Chairman of the White Star Line, Thomas Ismay, who lived nearby and did not want the railway on his land, saw to it that Thurstaston station was a considerable distance from the village it purported to serve, the two being linked by a footpath. This photograph, taken in October 2006, features the author, who had just walked part of the Wirral Way. Ismay's house, Dawpool, has long since been demolished, as have the station buildings. *R. Trill*

Below: Overgrown platform foundations still existed at Parkgate in 2007, together with this old cobbled path leading from the former station to the seafront. Ferry services between Parkgate and North Wales ended in the 1860s, but the resort was noted for its shrimps and became busy during holiday periods, with large crowds once descending to the nearby beach. The silting of the Dee estuary has continued, and a salt marsh has now replaced much of the original beach at Parkgate. *Author*

Right: The bridges on the original 1866 Hooton–Parkgate line, including this one at Neston, photographed in 2006, were built of sandstone, but on the later 1886 Parkgate–West Kirby section the bridges were brick-built. All the bridges were built to accommodate double track, yet even in the line's heyday, when it enjoyed a frequent service, this was never required. *Author*

Below: Hadlow Road station served the nearby village of Willaston and once employed a stationmaster and a signalman as well as booking clerks and porters. Following closure of the station in 1956 the station house building was occupied by a retired railwayman, thereby becoming the principal surviving railway structure on the line from Hooton to West Kirby. It is now a key visitor attraction on the Wirral Way, this view having been recorded in September 2006. *Author*

ERO27458

L.M. & S.R.

CALDY

Above left: Typical of the gas lights provided for the interior of stations is this survivor at Hadlow Road, photographed in September 2006. The pilot light to the right of the gas mantle allowed the light to be turned on and off by means of chains that once hung from the bar above the lamp, which in turn operated a gas valve. At one time, of a station staff of six, four would always be on duty between 6am and 11pm, their tasks including the lighting and maintenance of the station's gas lamps and their fragile asbestos mantles. *R. Trill*

Above centre: Highlighting the past. Some 40 milk churns were once despatched daily from Hadlow Road, an operation which in the winter months was carried out in darkness. This large distinctive gas light, optimally placed on the corner of the station building, provided useful platform illumination and would also have been appreciated by commuters. The lamp is seen here, minus its internal gas fittings, in September 2006. *R. Trill*

Above right: An example of a Sugg upright 'Rochester shadowless' type of gas light at Hadlow Road in September 2006. A glass globe was once provided under the wide-brimmed 'hat' which the LMS had fitted to existing gas lamp-posts throughout Merseyside. The station and its gas lamps have been well restored as an historic feature on the Wirral Way. *R. Trill*

Left: Photographed in September 2006, the brick waiting shelter on the down platform at Hadlow Road, which once afforded protection from the elements to railway passengers on this rural branch, is now of similar benefit to walkers using the Wirral Way. A similar structure once existed at Thurstaston. *Author*

15 Working the network

As the railway network grew, a succession of locomotive sheds was built to serve the area. These varied in size, functional design and equipment, and many specialised in terms of the duties undertaken (and consequently the classes of locomotive allocated). Most of the sheds were initially modest, but, as the network developed, many were extended, and in some cases huge concrete mechanical coaling stages were introduced; others, on restricted sites, notably at main-line termini, could not be expanded. Some of the more important sheds in the area are considered in this chapter.

Edge Hill was the most important Liverpool shed, particularly for express-passenger locomotives. One of the first sheds in the area, being able to trace its roots back to the L&MR, it was developed by the LNWR (which at one time had more than 100 locomotives allocated there) and considerably rebuilt by the LMS, and in BR days the shed (coded 8A) had 19 tracks and six through roads. It was also one of the last to close, in May 1968. The shed and associated structures were subsequently demolished.

Warrington Dallam (BR code 8B) was another ex-LNWR shed. In the 1950s there were about 60 locomotives allocated — mainly ex-LMS types engaged on freight duties in the area. The nine-track shed closed in October 1967, having outlasted smaller sheds at Warrington Arpley and Warrington Central.

Speke Junction shed (8C) opened in 1886, as a result of the growing use of the network in the Liverpool and Garston areas. Located in the triangle formed by the Runcorn–Liverpool and Garston Dock lines, this eventual 12-road facility housed about 60 locomotives, mainly freight types. Closure came in 1968.

Bank Hall (27A) was opened by the LYR in 1850, on land at the junction of the Preston and Southport lines. The facilities were modernised by the LMS, and until the 1950s as many as 40 locomotives could be found 'on shed'. The allocation comprised a variety of locomotives, including the small ex-LYR 0-4-0ST 'Pugs' used on the dock sidings. All structures were demolished following the shed's closure in October 1966, but the site was still used as an EMU depot in 2008.

Aintree's shed (No 19 of the LYR, and eventually BR's 27B) opened in 1886 and specialised in freight workings from the docks. The LMS added a mechanical coaling plant (in 1937) and an electric turntable to the eventual eight-road shed. For many years the locomotive allocation hovered at around 50, but by the end this had reduced to just three.

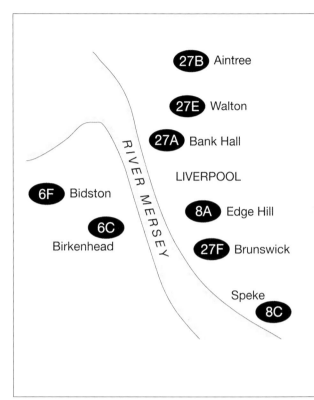

Closure came in June 1967, when two of the remaining locomotives were transferred to Warrington Dallam.

Opened in 1879 to serve the CLC and Liverpool Central station, the five-road Brunswick shed was on a relatively difficult and cramped site, its construction having involved much rock excavation. The majority of the motive power was provided initially by the GCR and later the LNER, but latterly the allocation comprised largely ex-LMS types. Very run-down towards the end, the shed (BR code 8E, changed to 27F in 1958) closed in September 1961 and was subsequently demolished, although a considerable length of outer wall remained in 2008.

Walton-on-the-Hill (27E) was the smaller of the two main CLC sheds in the Liverpool area. Opened in 1881, it was rebuilt in 1952 but thereafter became less used, with only about 20 locomotives allocated. Ex-CLC locomotives were gradually replaced by LMS types. Closed in December 1963, the shed was later demolished, and the site is now occupied by a housing development.

Birkenhead shed, sometimes also known as Mollington Street (6C; 8H from 1963), served Woodside station and Birkenhead Docks and had been opened in 1879 jointly by the GWR and LNWR, which built adjoining separate sheds. Nationalisation resulted in joint use of the facilities, but in 1951 the entire shed was taken over by the LMR. In 1959 it housed 56 locomotives of some 16 different class types, including many of GWR origin, and upon its closure in November 1967 some 47 steam locomotives were still to be found 'on shed'. The buildings continued in use as a diesel depot until November 1985, finally being demolished in 1987.

The two-road shed at Bidston, on the Wirral peninsula, was opened in 1897 by the Manchester, Sheffield & Lincolnshire Railway, which soon became part of the GCR. Freight-orientated, the shed (BR code 6F) closed in February 1963, its demise prompted by the decline of freight and the spread of 'dieselisation'. The remaining BR Standard Class 9 2-10-0s, used extensively on iron-ore trains, were transferred to Birkenhead Mollington Street, and the site was duly redeveloped.

At Southport the ex-LYR shed at Derby Road (27C) closed in 1966 to become a railway preservation centre, 'Steamport', which duly opened in 1974. This itself closed in 1991, and the former locomotive shed has since been demolished. The preservation centre had contained many items from the area, including the signalbox from Riverside station, the Mersey Railway locomotive *Cecil Raikes* and an LOR coach. Much of the stock has been transferred to the Ribble Steam Railway at Preston, although other items have been more widely dispersed.

Below: A mix of locomotive types congregate by the concrete coaling stage at Edge Hill shed on 29 July 1953. Ex-LNWR 'G2' (LMS '7F') 0-8-0 No 49445 and ex-LMS '3F' 0-6-0T No 47416 stand beneath the coal chute as 'WD' 2-8-0 No 90566 draws onto the pits. The LNWR had enlarged the site in 1864 and 1902 and provided enhanced coaling facilities in 1914, and the shed was further rebuilt and expanded by the LMS. *R. Hewitt*

Right: Edge Hill in 1952, with Class 8P 'Princess' Pacific No 46202 *Princess Anne* in view. Built in 1935, this locomotive had run successfully as a turbine engine until 1952, when it was rebuilt with conventional cylinders and named. Its life in rebuilt form would be short, this being the locomotive destroyed in the Harrow railway disaster in October of the same year. *Eric Treacy*

Centre right: Edge Hill in the late 1950s, with another of the Class 8P 'Princess' Pacifics, No 46208 *Princess Helena Victoria*, in BR livery. The locomotive, built by the LMS in 1935, is seen topping up with coal before heading souith to Euston with the 'Merseyside Express', which was timed at around 3½ hours, running non-stop. This train had been introduced by the LMS in 1927 as the 'London–Merseyside Express', the name being shortened in 1932. *Eric Treacy*

Right: By the 1950s Edge Hill had become the largest shed in the Liverpool area. This view, recorded *c*1960, features Class 8P 'Duchess' Pacific No 46229 *Duchess of Hamilton*. As built, by the LMS in 1938, this locomotive had been clad in streamlined casing and in 1939, masquerading as No 6220 *Coronation*, was exhibited in the USA, returning to Britain in 1943. It is now preserved. *J. Carter*

Left: The 10-road Warrington Dallam shed was located on the west side of the West Coast main line, about a mile north of Warrington Bank Quay station, close to the CLC line. Among the locomotives on shed on 1 July 1965 were Stanier 'Black Five' 4-6-0s Nos 45041 and 45442, Class 9F 2-10-0 No 92119, an unidentified 'Jinty' 0-6-0T and, third from right, Stanier 'Jubilee' 4-6-0 No 45563 *Australia. W. Ballard*

Below left: Another view of Warrington Dallam shed, with Stanier 'Black Five' 4-6-0 No 45323 raising steam, on 27 September 1967. Also present are two BR/Sulzer Type 2 (Class 25) diesel locomotives, the photograph being taken shortly before closure of the steam shed. The sub-shed at Warrington Arpley station had closed in 1963. *J. Cooper-Smith*

Bottom left: Still in LMS livery but displaying its new BR number, an ex-LYR 0-4-0ST 'Pug' dating from 1905 stands at Bank Hall shed on 18 April 1950. At this time Bank Hall could field a dozen 'Pugs', which helped maintain the shed's LYR atmosphere well after nationalisation. The last would be withdrawn by 1962. *R. M. Casserley*

Right: Bank Hall shed on 22 August 1960. Under the huge concrete coaling tower is BR Class 6 Pacific No 72006 *Clan Mackenzie*, contrasting with diminutive ex-LYR 'Pug' 0-4-0ST No 51232 waiting its turn. The 'Clan' was based at Carlisle and had arrived in Liverpool at the head of an Anglo-Scottish express. It would be withdrawn in 1966. *Ian Allan Library*

Above: Brunswick shed in LNER days, with 'D6' No 5268, an ex-GCR 4-4-0 of 1897, fitted with Ramsbottom safety valves. The locomotive was allocated to Liverpool and Stockport for most of the pre-WW2 period. As can be seen, much of the site was hewn out of sandstone. The shed was to close in 1961. *LPC*

Below: Aintree shed on 5 November 1960, with the last ex-LYR 0-6-0T, No 51537, complete with chimney cowl. After the 1923 Grouping the LYR shed code was retained for a while, but the number was prefixed by the letter 'C' to denote the Central division of the LMS, before a more standard coding was introduced. After closure the derelict building, located in the fork of the Ford–Aintree and Ford–Kirkby lines, would remain intact for almost 30 years, becoming known locally as the 'Ghosty'. *L. Sandler*

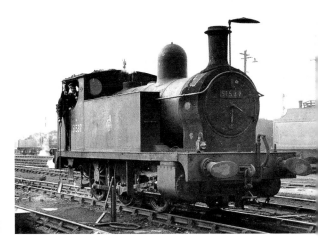

Above: Birkenhead shed in 1966, with, from left to right, Class 8F 2-8-0 No 48199 (with the '9F' code of Heaton Mersey shed painted on its smokebox door) and BR Class 9F 2-10-0s Nos 92021 (with Franco-Crosti boiler) and 92082. All three locomotives are simmering away, giving a clue to the shed's importance for freight work at this time, but would be withdrawn the following year. *Ian Allan Library*

Left: Birkenhead shed was located on a short spur from Green Lane Junction on the Woodside line. Differences between the adjoining ex-LMS and ex-GWR sheds could still be discerned, long after nationalisation, when the shed was operated as a single depot. This scene, recorded on 28 January 1984, reflects the conversion to diesel traction, with three types of locomotive in view. From left to right are Class 25 No 25 199, Class 40 No 40 195 and Class 47s Nos 47 104 and 47 301. *J. Augustson*

Left: Class 25s Nos 25 226 and 25 307 at Birkenhead shed on 17 April 1984. It finally closed as a diesel depot in 1985. *J. Augustson*

Right: The six-road shed at Southport was located to the east of Chapel Street station, on the north side of the ex-LYR line from Wigan. The shed code changed from 23C to 27C in 1950, and again to 8M in 1963. A trio of Stanier 'Black Fives' lurk within its murky depths in March 1965. It was from this shed that the last ex-LYR 2-4-2T had worked until February 1961. *M. Baker*

Below right: A trio of industrial 0-4-0ST locomotives at Southport shed on 12 September 1982, during the Steamport era. From left to right are a Peckett, dating from 1941 and once used by the Southport Gas Co, a Hudswell Clarke dating from 1906, and *Efficient*, a Barclay dating from 1918 and once used at a copper-smelting works at Widnes. The shed has since been demolished, but the locomotives can still be found at other railway preservation centres. *D. Rawlinson*

Below: Alongside a solid-looking water crane, Stanier 2-6-0 No 42953, turned out by the LMS in 1933, stands on shed at Southport in June 1965. Closed by BR the following year, the shed would endure a period of dereliction pending reuse by Steamport (from 1971). *M. Baker*

Below right: A disused locomotive water tank, by now supporting some small trees, was still extant at Edge Hill in September 2006. The original steam sheds have been demolished, but traces of the steam age can still be found throughout the area. *Author*

Gone with the St Helens & Runcorn Gap

By 1757 a navigable canal had been created by deepening the Sankey Brook, and this eventually linked St Helens, with its plentiful supplies of coal and sand, to the River Mersey, prompting William Pilkington to establish his glass works in the town in 1826. In February 1833 the St Helens & Runcorn Gap Railway, aiming to break the canal's monopoly, officially opened a more direct 8-mile single line to convey coal from pits in the St Helens area to the Mersey at Runcorn Gap, now known as Widnes.

In 1836 the L&MR ran to the south of St Helens, and an elegant iron-and-stone bridge was built to allow the freight line to cross over the L&MR to the

west of what was to become St Helens Junction station. The St Helens line was a very early railway, and its main function was to convey coal. There were initially no passenger stations, but soon a couple of coaches were hired from the L&MR and attached to the rear of some coal trains.

To compete with the new railway the canal reduced its rates. Eventually the two agreed upon a merger, resulting in the formation in 1845 of the St Helens Canal & Railway. Initially some of the line's steeper gradients had been rope-hauled, but these were later eased to allow locomotive haulage throughout. The reinvigorated company was also able to extend the railway 5½ miles northward from

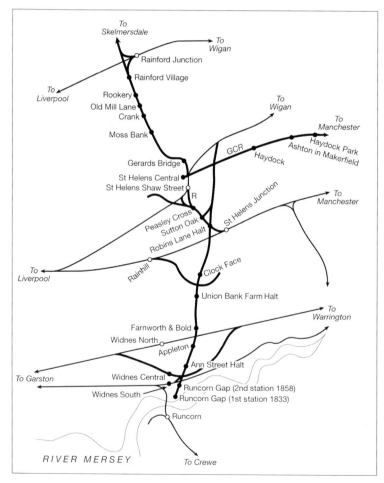

Right: The historic crossing of the St Helens & Runcorn Gap Railway over the L&MR, an Ericsson 'Novelty'-type locomotive passing over a Stephenson 'Northumbrian' (left). The ex-L&MR double-track line at the lower level here is still open, but the railway over it, engineered by Charles Vignoles, closed in 1981. The bridge has been rebuilt, but the location can still be readily identified today. *Liverpool Record Office, Liverpool Libraries*

St Helens to Rainford Junction. Furthermore, as the original dock at Runcorn Gap was experiencing difficulties due to shifting sands, a new line via Speke to Garston Dock was opened in 1852.

The original line was doubled and became one of the busiest coal freight lines in the North West. Although passenger services remained less important, the original station at St Helens was replaced by 1858 with a new station, allowing through services to Rainford Junction. At the other end of the line a new station, also called Runcorn Gap but more convenient to Widnes, opened in 1852, resulting in the closure of the original.

In 1864 all the lines were absorbed by the LNWR, which then became a dock owner outside Liverpool, promoting Garston Dock with the slogan 'Coal her at Garston'. Improvements were made at Widnes, including a link to the Widnes Deviation — a new, elevated east–west line that avoided crossing existing lines and roads on the level. A new station at Widnes (later called Widnes South) was opened on this line in 1870. Ann Street and Union Bank Farm halts were also added to the St Helens line by the LNWR in 1911, and a number of rail-motor services were introduced.

St Helens Shaw Street (as it would be known from 1949) had become the centre of a network of lines serving the town and the coalfield, including the link to the erstwhile L&MR at St Helens Junction.

The GCR had its own line to St Helens Central station, and passenger services to Manchester had commenced in January 1900. However, in the years following World War 2 the area's fortunes declined with those of the coalfield, and the network began to contract. The GCR line closed to passengers in March 1952, but Haydock Park station continued to open on race days until the line's closure to remaining freight traffic in 1965. The author's diary for 1967 recalls the contraction of the rail network in this area at the time:

St Helens station is new, but four tracks had been replaced by two. The line had a mixture of old and new signals, and some parts were still on ash ballast. Numerous closed industrial links and lines were noted.

After many years as a heavily used freight route the Widnes–St Helens Shaw Street line had closed to passengers in July 1951, together with the link to Rainford Junction. Passenger trains ran on from Rainford Junction to Skelmersdale until November 1956, and some freight continued to use the Rainford Junction–St Helens Shaw Street section until 1967; St Helens Junction–St Helens Shaw Street passenger trains also used part of the line until June 1965. The Widnes–St Helens Shaw Street line remained as a through freight route until November 1981, the track (much of which had

already been singled) being lifted the following year. However, the St Helens Shaw Street–Sutton Oak Junction section remained open for freight until 1986, and the last 1-mile section south of St Helens Shaw Street similarly until September 2002.

Returning to St Helens in 2007, some 40 years after his first visit, the author was struck to discover how much remained relatively unchanged. The surviving line to the town still had a mixture of old semaphore and new signals, an industrial atmosphere was still evident, and at the station even the tracks towards Widnes remained *in situ*. Moreover, in contrast to the complete closure that

was threatened in 1967, plans for improvement and a possible reopening to St Helens Junction were in prospect.

At Widnes the original stations and dock sidings have been lost, while the swing bridge over the St Helens Canal was demolished in the early 1980s, but traces of the Widnes South station of 1870 can still be found. Elsewhere, the closed trackbed still crosses over the erstwhile L&MR by two bridges (albeit not in original form) just west of St Helens Junction. None of the closed intermediate stations survives intact, but parts of the historic route are used as roads or footpaths.

Right: BR Standard Class 2 2-6-0 No 78035 pauses near Clock Face on 2 March 1962 with the 2.55pm Pilkington's Sidings–Widnes freight. Having been detached from its train the locomotive would proceed up the colliery branch to pick up wagons before continuing its journey. *Ian Allan Library*

Below: Class 25s Nos 25 287 and 25 113 head away from St Helens Shaw Street towards St Helens Junction on 29 June 1977 with a train of empty oil tankers bound for Ellesmere Port. Although disused, the track and signalling here still remained in 2007, as did the similarly disused canal. *P. Hanson*

Right: Headed by an ex-LMS 0-6-0 running tender-first, the Locomotive Club of Great Britain's 'South Lancashire Ltd' railtour calls at St Helens Central station on 21 September 1963. Unlike St Helens Shaw Street, which remains open and is now just called St Helens, the terminus of the ex-GCR branch from Lowton St Mary's (which never formed part of the St Helens–Runcorn Gap route) was a very modest affair. Regular passenger services ceased in March 1952, to be followed in January 1965 by the remaining freight. *Ian Holt*

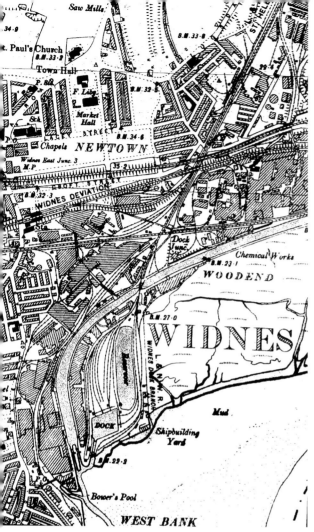

ST. HELENS, ST. HELENS JUNCTION, and WARRINGTON.—London and North Western.

Miles.	Down. Shaw Street Station,	Week Days.																					
		mrn	mrn	mrn	mrn	mrn	mrn	mrn		aft	n	aft	aft	aft	aft	aft	aft	aft	aft	aft	aft
	St. Helens..............dep.	6 55	8 0	8 30	9 0	9 10	1025	1110	Tues.	12 5	1220	1 0	1 45	2 50	3 35	4 27	5 25	5 40	6 20	6 55	7 20
¼	Peasley Cross............	6 58		8 33		9 13	1028	1113		12 8	1223	1 3	1 48	2 53	3 38		5 28		6 23	6 58	7 23
1¼	Sutton Oak............	7 1	8 4	8 36		9 16	1031	1116		1211	1226	1 6	1 51	2 56	3 41	4 31	5 31		6 26	7 1	7 26
2	St. Helens Junc. 494, 496 arr.	7 3	8 6	8 38	9 8	9 19	1033	1118		1213	1228	1 8	1 53	2 58	3 43	4 34	5 33	5 45	6 28	7 3	7 28
9¾	494 Warrington (Bank Q.) arr.	7 22	8 54	9 1	9 25			1134			1 25	2 21	3 35		5 0	5 55		7 3		8 20	

Down. Shaw Street Station,	Week Days—Continued.				Sundays.						
	aft	aft		aft	aft		mrn	aft	aft	aft	
St. Helens..............dep.	8 50	1025		1040	1135		7 50	6 55	9 5	1025	
Peasley Cross............	8 53	1028	Sats.	1043			7 53	6 58	9 8		
Sutton Oak............	8 56	1031		1046 Sat.			7 56	7 1	9 11		
St. Helens Junc. 494, 496 arr.	8 59	1033		1048	1141		7 58	7 3	9 13	1031	
494 Warrington (Bank Q.) arr.	9 26	11½0		11 5	1210s		8 39	7 35	1119 o		

Miles.	Up. Bank Quay Station,	Week Days.																			
		mrn	mrn	mrn	mrn	mrn	mrn	aft		aft	aft	aft	aft	aft	aft	aft	aft	aft	aft	aft
	496 Warrington ....dep.	7 11		8 23	9 19	1015	1055		1225	2 45	3 45			5 15			6 37	7 8	7 40		
	St. Helens Junction ....dep.	7 35	8 15	8 53	9 47	1033	12 0	1230	1250	Sats.	1 25	2 28	3 4	8 4	4 48	5 10	5 52	6 33	6 55	7 44	8 18
¾	Sutton Oak............	7 38	8 18	8 56	9 50	1036	12 3	1233	1253		1 28	2 30	3 7	4 9		5 13	5 55		6 58	7 47	8 18
1¼	Peasley Cross............	7 41	8 21	9 1		1039	12 6	1236	1255		1 31	2 33	3 10	4 12		5 53		7 1	7 50	8 22	
2	St. Helens (Shaw St.) 483.arr.	7 43	8 23	9 3	9 54	1041	12 8	1238	1258		1 35	2 35	3 12	4 14	4 52	5 16	6 0	6 38	7 3	7 52	8 23

Up. Bank Quay Station,	Week Days—Continued.				Sundays.			
	aft	aft	aft	aft		mrn	aft	aft	aft
496 Warrington ....dep.	9 30	1035	1148			S 35	6 0	10 8	
St. Helens Junction ......dep.	9 55	11 0	1210			8 55	7 35	9 28	1045
Sutton Oak............	9 23	9 58	11 3			8 58	7 38	9 31	
Peasley Cross............	9 26	10 1	11 6			9 1	7 41	9 34	
St. Helens (Shaw St.) 483.arr.	9 28	10 3	11 9	1217		9 3	7 43	9 36	1053

a Except Tuesdays.   o Via Newton-le-Willows.   s Saturdays only.

Far left: Map of the railway lines at Widnes in 1895. Note also the disused St Helens Canal, which, unlike the railway to St Helens, survives today. *Crown Copyright*

Left: A surviving signal on the line south from St Helens Shaw Street station to St Helens Junction, photographed in September 2006. At this point the line crosses the upper section of the St Helens Canal by means of a solid brick causeway that for many years has precluded use of this stretch of the canal. *Author's collection*

Below left: St Helens Shaw Street– St Helens Junction timetable, April 1910. Note the two intermediate stations provided on the 2-mile route. Robins Lane Halt would be added by the LMS in 1936 but closed in 1938.

Top right: A shuttle service was operated between St Helens Shaw Street and St Helens Junction, on the ex-L&MR line. The latter station remains open, but the platform for Shaw Street, seen here in September 2006, has not been used since the withdrawal of passenger services in 1965. Plans to reinstate the link to Shaw Street have yet to come to fruition. *Author*

Centre right: The historic crossing of the one-time St Helens & Runcorn Gap Railway over the erstwhile L&MR remains *in situ*. One of the two bridges that replaced the original structure is seen here in September 2006. *Author's collection*

Right: The Sankey Brook was developed as England's first commercial canal, featuring the first double locks, and became known as the St Helens Canal. At Widnes, where it was crossed by the railway, a swing bridge was required to permit its continued use by sailing barges. The bridge has now been removed, but the pivotal seating pit is seen here, in September 2006. *Author*

17 A line in the road

Birkenhead was the home of the first street tramway in Europe, the horse-worked line being opened in August 1860 by none other than George Francis Train. In later years trams were built at Birkenhead and exported from the port. The tram system was electrified in 1901, and an extensive network developed in both Birkenhead and Wallasey.

In Liverpool a short line opened in 1862 but closed the following year. A tramway company was finally established, and the city centre and Dingle routes were constructed, the first horse trams operating by 1869. In 1897 most of the tram companies in the Liverpool area were taken over by Liverpool Corporation, and between 1898 and 1902 the tram network was electrified.

Southport, St Helens and Warrington also had tram systems, and all were converted to electric traction. The fact that it was possible to travel into deepest Lancashire on the area's many tram lines prompted the suggestion that the network be used to transport goods, and an experimental trip was made from Liverpool to Bolton. However, concerns over noise, particularly at night, and the disruption

likely to be caused during the day to intensively used passenger services ensured that the experiment came to nothing.

The first trams to run in the middle of the road in Britain were introduced in Liverpool in 1914, while the outbreak of World War 1 saw women take over the working of many services, the remaining men being issued with badges to indicate that theirs was a reserved occupation. Prior to this, in 1908, special all-First-class trams, painted in a distinctive livery, had been introduced on some routes, but passengers resented paying First-class fares to travel on the upper deck, and the cars in question reverted to standard in 1923.

The LOR operated its own Seaforth Sands–Great Crosby tram link. Opened in 1900, this line was the first significant electric tram line to close in the Merseyside area, in 1925. Wallasey's tram services ended in 1933, Southport and Warrington trams were the next to go, in 1935, and those at St Helens followed in 1936. The Birkenhead network was closed in July 1937; tramcar No 22 was specially illuminated for the final day, and a driver who had

Left: Part of the route of the Storeton Tramway under the Birkenhead–Chester line at Port Sunlight, long since converted to a footpath, seen here in October 2006. This mineral tramway was laid early in the 1800s and until 1902 was used to transport building stone from quarries to the tidal creek at Bromborough. On the right of the picture can be seen part of the Lever Bros soap factory, which once had its own railway, used to transport workers to Bromborough.
Author

Above: In June 1900 the Liverpool Overhead Railway introduced its own service between Seaforth Sands station and Great Crosby — a distance of 2½ miles. This photograph shows one of the 14 green-and-cream tramcars used. The contrast between the spartan seats on the upper deck and the plush, curtained interior will be noted, as will the sign warning passengers not to climb the stairs until the car stops, while just discernible on the lower panels is the address of the LOR's James Street offices, destined to be destroyed during World War 2. *Ian Allan Library*

started with the horse-drawn trams was chosen for the sad last trip.

Liverpool, in contrast, retained and improved its trams. During World War 2 the trams, now painted in camouflage colours, were used to transport troops from Lime Street to the docks. Prisoners of war were also conveyed by tram, the windows being blacked out to prevent them from seeing the damage inflicted by air raids on the city.

Postwar the Liverpool tram system was in a run-down state, while in 1947 a fire at Green Lane depot destroyed about 10% of the stock, including many of the newer trams. Consequently a conversion to buses was agreed in 1948. At the end of World War 2 there had been about 750 vehicles, but the types and numbers of trams in use swiftly reduced, and by 1953

only 220 remained. Liverpool's last trams ran on 14 September 1957, an era of the city's transport history ending with a ceremonial procession at Pier Head. The tram lines were subsequently taken up, including the two circular track layouts at Pier Head.

Although the tram network at Southport closed in 1935, a tramway on the pier remains. The original pier at Southport — the second-longest in Britain — was the first real pleasure pier and was opened in 1860. To carry luggage along the 1,098yd structure a narrow-gauge cable tramway operated between 1863 and 1905, when electric traction replaced cable haulage. In 1935 new electric stock was provided, but the tramway closed in 1950 after the electricity supply was nationalised, it proving impracticable to convert the tram motors, which ran on direct current, to work on the new alternating current. The pier tramway was thus replaced by a diesel-operated 2ft-gauge tramway of reduced length, which itself closed in the 1990. In 2005 a new, two-car tram was introduced on a rebuilt 3ft 6in-gauge pier tramway.

Four former Liverpool trams survive, including one in the USA, whilst the Wirral Transport Museum at Birkenhead provides a fascinating history of the tram systems in the Merseyside area. Its collection includes original trams from Liverpool, Birkenhead, Wallasey and Warrington, all of which operate over a section of tramway to the Woodside ferry terminal.

Above right: Liverpool Corporation tram No 138 on route 43A to Pier Head. In the background can be seen the CLC line to Aintree; on the overbridge (and giving a clue to the date of the photograph) is a sign to Clubmoor station, opened in 1927 to serve new suburbs in the area. *Liverpool Record Office, Liverpool Libraries*

Below: Road congestion near Pier Head in 1957, as a horse-drawn cart loaded with sacks from the docks prevents a Corporation bus bound for Dingle from reaching its stop. A faster service to Dingle was provided by the LOR, looming in the background but by now closed. *K. Swallow*

Right: On 14 September 1957 Liverpool's last 26 trams ran in service for the final time from Edge Lane depot. The last in regular service was No 274 on route 40, while the specially painted 'Last Tram' was No 293. This was the scene at Pier Head, where a large crowd had gathered to say goodbye to the city's 'Green Goddesses'. At 6pm all the ships in the Mersey sounded their horns in a farewell salute, and then, with a police escort, the trams returned in a solemn convoy to the depot, which they entered to the strains of 'Auld Lang Syne'. *Liverpool Record Office, Liverpool Libraries*

Above right: Birkenhead was home to the first British tramway, and trams were later built there, so it is fitting that an operational tramway now links the Woodside Ferry terminal with the Wirral Transport Museum in Taylor Street. The route involves street running by trams such as Birkenhead No 20, built by Milnes in 1900 and pictured in September 2006. In the background can be seen the ex-MeR pumping station, which retains its mighty beam engine. *Author*

Right: Two of the electric cars introduced in 1935 on Southport's narrow-gauge pier tramway, destined to close in 1950, when the electricity supply was changed. Itself closed in the late 1990s for safety reasons, the pier has since been rebuilt, and a new tramway of 3ft 6in gauge was opened in 2005. *W. Garth*

18 Miniature pleasures past and present

Not all the railways in the area were built primarily for industrial purposes; some lines were built purely for fun and pleasure, and these have ranged from fairground helter-skelters to elaborate miniature networks.

A well-liked miniature railway was once to be found alongside the promenade at New Brighton. The line was built by Tommy Man, who purchased much of the 18in-gauge equipment from Jaywick, the miniature line in Essex having closed upon the outbreak of World War 2. A further steam locomotive was purchased in 1950, and a new station opened in 1952. The miniature steam locomotives and enclosed coaches were a popular attraction during the summer months. However, in the late 1950s and early '60s the number of holidaymakers visiting New Brighton declined, and the railway closed at the end of the 1965 summer season.

A miniature railway on a much larger scale was to be found at the Liverpool International Garden Festival. The first event of its kind in Britain, this was conceived as a means of regenerating part of the derelict south docks. Gardens, lakes and trees apart, one of its main features was an extensive and elaborate 15in miniature railway network, complete with a depot, bridges, stations and colour-light signalling. The railway was opened on 2 May 1984 by HM The Queen, travelling in a Royal Train.

The Garden Festival railway used stock from existing miniature railways. The locomotive, *Samson*, and coaches were hired from the Romney, Hythe & Dymchurch Railway (RH&DR). The stock included a standard 20-seater enclosed saloon that was converted to a splendid Royal saloon for use by the Royal party on the opening of the line. Three key items of stock were also hired from the Ravenglass & Eskdale Railway (R&ER) — the locomotive *River Irt*, the diesel *Shelagh* (used to haul the Royal Train on the opening day) and a three-car diesel multiple-unit.

The Garden Festival railway was heavily used and a great success but was dismantled following closure of the Festival in October 1984. Much of the railway material, including some stations, was purchased by a theme park near Ilkeston, which in 1985 opened a 15in-gauge railway, but this has since closed. However, most of the rolling stock that was used on the Garden Festival railway can still be seen back on the R&ER and RH&DR lines. A sizeable proportion of the Garden Festival site has remained in a derelict

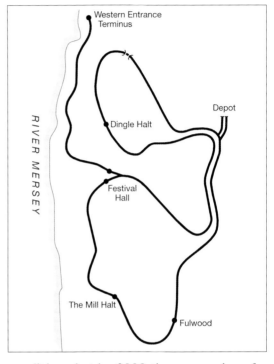

condition, but by 2008 there were plans for regeneration, although these did not include a miniature railway.

Not all the original pleasure lines are lost. Opened in 1911, the Lakeside Miniature Railway at Southport, running from Pleasure Land to the pier, was extended to Peter Pan's Pool in time for the 1949 summer season. The extension prompted the closure in 1948 of Princes Park station, although the overgrown and derelict station building can still be seen on the miniature railway, which, in contrast to the brief existence of the Garden Festival line, is the oldest continually running miniature railway in the world.

While on the subject of pleasure railways, it is of note that very small trains were also once manufactured in Liverpool. Frank Hornby, a Liverpudlian, began producing clockwork trains after World War 1, the first being sold in the 1920s as construction kits. They were soon being sold already assembled, and later the Hornby electric train sets became world-famous. Hornby remains a byword for model railways today.

Left: Layout of the miniature railway provided for the Liverpool International Garden Festival.

Above: The Liverpool International Garden Festival site on 26 April 1984, with extensive tree-planting evident. *River Irt*, a 15in-gauge miniature 0-8-2 steam locomotive loaned from the Ravenglass & Eskdale Railway (R&ER) in Cumbria, heads a test train near the Chinese garden. *A. Bowler*

Right: The inclusion of a miniature railway added real excitement to the Garden Festival project. Steam locomotives, supplemented by diesel traction, worked intensive passenger services over the 15in miniature pleasure line. *River Irt* pauses at Fulwood station on 12 June 1984. *R. Ruffell*

Right: River Irt on 16 June 1984, with huge crowds waiting to take the train. This is the world's oldest working 15in-gauge locomotive, its Heywood-built chassis dating from 1894. *D. Rowe*

Left: Samson, a 4-8-2 built by Davey Paxman in 1926 and loaned from the 15in-gauge Romney, Hythe & Dymchurch Railway (RH&DR) in Kent, arrives at one of the festival's stations on a wet 12 June 1984. Some 3.4 million people visited the Garden Festival, and the railway was a huge success. *R. Ruffell*

Below left: Samson leaves Fulwood station and passes under a wooden suspension bridge on 8 July 1984. This was one of several bridges on the line, and there was even a short tunnel. *B. Dobbs*

Top right: The Festival site was reclaimed from derelict dockland near Dingle. Maintaining the maritime theme, *River Irt* passes the 'SS *Ty-Phoo*' on 8 August 1984. This view shows to good advantage the locomotive's 0-8-2 wheel arrangement and unique Heywood valvegear. *N. Hunt*

Above right: The 'Silver Jubilee' train at Festival Hall station on 26 April 1984. On loan from the R&ER, this three-car diesel unit, with centre coach modified to facilitate disabled access, was used to provide a shuttle service to the main entrance. The railway carried over a million passengers in the first four months of the Garden Festival, which was open from 2 May to 14 October 1984. *A. Bowler*

Right: Upon closure of the festival the railway track, along with much of the infrastructure, was sold, and the site has since become overgrown. However, part of a footbridge could still be found in September 2007. *Author*

19 Railway hotels

The Lime Street Hotel, adjoining Lime Street station, provides Liverpool's skyline with one of its most distinctive outlines. Designed by Alfred Waterhouse and with an opulent interior decorated in French Renaissance style to match the exterior, this huge building was the city's first purpose-built railway hotel, having been opened by the LNWR in 1871. However, with 200 bedrooms but just eight baths, it was also the first to close, business being transferred by the LMS to the more modern Adelphi in March 1933. Thereafter the stone building became ever more blackened and decayed, water seeping in and ruining much of the ornate plasterwork and ceilings, and by 1977 it was largely disused. Happily it has since been restored, reopening in 1996 for use as student accommodation.

The Exchange Hotel, built for the LYR and opened in August 1888, was more modest in size but with 80 bedrooms and extensive facilities was properly considered a luxury hotel. Built in a free

Renaissance style, this elegant stone-fronted building, which enjoyed direct access to/from Exchange station, also gained some business from the Lime Street Hotel as part of rationalisation by the LMS in the 1930s. It closed in July 1971, but fortunately the stone frontage was retained when the main trainsheds were demolished in 1977, after closure of the station, and has since been cleaned and incorporated in a new office development.

The current Adelphi Hotel, opened in 1914, was the third hotel on the site. It was built for the Midland Railway, which for a time, to promote its new hotel, ran trains non-stop from St Pancras to the nearby Central station. Designed by Frank Atkinson, this imposing building was of modern construction for its day and, with its elegant rooms and marble-lined corridors, was certainly worthy of a great commercial city like Liverpool; indeed, upon its opening it was described by the *Liverpool Daily Post* as the world's greatest hotel.

Below left: The magnificent symmetrical façade of the Lime Street Hotel, as it was once generally known, photographed in April 2006. In style a mixture of baronial hall and French château, it remains one of Liverpool's most impressive buildings. *Author*

LIME STREET HOTEL

(UNDER THE MANAGEMENT OF THE L. & N. W. RLY. CO.),

ADJOINS LIME STREET STATION.

One of the largest and most comfortable Hotels in Liverpool.

RECENTLY RE-DECORATED AND RE-FURNISHED.

Over 300 Bed and Sitting Rooms.

Spacious Dining, Drawing, Smoking, and Billiard Rooms.

Finely appointed Banqueting Hall and Luxurious Lounge.

HAIRDRESSING SALOON, POST OFFICE, and TYPEWRITING ROOM in the HOTEL.

Hotel Porters in uniform meet all Trains.

TARIFF EXTREMELY MODERATE, CUISINE EXCELLENT, AND WINES OF THE FINEST QUALITY.

Electric Light throughout. Lifts to all Floors.

GARAGE. Telegraphic Address:—"RESTOTEL, LIVERPOOL."

National Telephone, private branch, exchange to all parts of the Hotel (6 lines). Telephone No. 2960 Royal.

THE Hotel is specially appointed for the convenience of American Travellers, as it adjoins the most important Railway Station in Liverpool, from which there are Trains to London (Euston) performing the journey in under four hours; forty minutes hourly service of Trains to Manchester; and Through Trains to Leeds, York, Hull, Newcastle, the Lakes, Scotland, Chester, the North Wales Coast, Bristol, Birmingham, and all parts of England.

Right: Advertisement for the Lime Street Hotel, 1910.

Right: The lofty main stairwell of the erstwhile Lime Street Hotel, photographed in April 2006. The iron girders supporting the staircase were restored with assistance from the Railway Heritage Trust. The hotel was once heated by steam, which also powered the luggage lifts, and enjoyed direct access to Liverpool Lime Street station. *Author*

The Adelphi was much in demand during the period of transatlantic liner travel from Liverpool, much being made of this by the LMS, and despite being damaged in World War 2 it went on to become a well-known Liverpool institution. It was sold out of railway ownership in 1983 but remains open.

While Liverpool could boast three principal railway-built hotels (the only city outside London and Glasgow to be so endowed), its massive growth was such that no fewer than seven other, smaller railway-owned hotels were transferred to the LMS in

1923. All were subsequently sold out of railway ownership, and most are long closed.

On the Wirral coast, the huge Hydro Hotel at West Kirby was completed in 1896. This was not railway-owned, but West Kirby was heavily promoted by the Wirral Railway as a seaside health resort and holiday destination. The hotel has since been demolished, but a railway to West Kirby survives. Finally on the Wirral coast, the castle at Leasowe was converted in 1910 into a home for retired railwaymen. This closed in 1970, but the building is now used as a hotel.

Above: The elegant clock on the frontage of the ex-LYR Exchange Hotel, seen in January 1965. The entrance, out of view to the left, was more modest. The building was described in Baedeker's guide as 'handsome', the only railway-owned building in Liverpool to be given such an accolade. Fortunately plans to demolish this part of the station were not implemented, and the attractive hotel façade and clock in Tithebarn Street were retained. *J. Clarke*

Above: The frontage of the Exchange Hotel features a plaque to John Pearson. Chairman of the LYR from 1883 to 1887, he was also at various times Mayor of Liverpool and High Sheriff of Lancashire, which fact emphasises the close links between the LYR and local authorities. *Author*

Right: Advertisement for the Exchange Hotel, 1910.

LANCASHIRE AND YORKSHIRE RAILWAY
EXCHANGE STATION HOTEL

| TELEGRAPHIC ADDRESS: "STATION HOTEL, LIVERPOOL." | **LIVERPOOL** | TELEPHONES: Nos. 3310 & 3311. |

UNDER THE MANAGEMENT OF THE COMPANY).

NEAREST FIRST-CLASS HOTEL TO THE TOWN HALL, LANDING STAGE, EXCHANGES, AND PRINCIPAL CENTRES OF BUSINESS.

Large Banqueting Hall and Grill Rooms.

Lighted throughout by Electricity.

THE HOTEL OFFERS EVERY ACCOMMODATION FOR VISITORS AND FAMILIES AT MODERATE CHARGES.

Rooms may be Telegraphed for, FREE OF CHARGE, from any principal Station on the Railway, on application to the Station Master or Telegraph Clerk.

Further particulars can be had on application to THE MANAGER.

Right: British Transport Hotels advertisement for the Adelphi, 1956. Nationalised in 1948, the hotel would be sold out of railway ownership in the 1980s. By the time of sale it was in poor condition, the top two floors being derelict, and closure was a real possibility, but happily it has since been restored to its former grandeur.

Below: Replacing an earlier and smaller hotel dating from 1876 (which in turn had replaced the 1826 original), the Adelphi Hotel that opened its doors in March 1914 was an eight-storey steel-framed structure clad in Portland stone and could boast no fewer than 600 bedrooms. Its sheer size is readily apparent from this view, recorded in April 2006. *Author*

LIVERPOOL (cont.).

Lime Street Station Hotel, Liverpool.—Owned and managed by the L.M & S.R. Company. Situated at Lime Street Station. The Hotel is specially appointed for the convenience of American travellers, as it adjoins the most important railway stations in Liverpool. Porters in Red Coats meet all principal trains, and remove luggage to and from the Hotel without charge. Telegraphic address: " Bestotel, Liverpool." Telephone No. Royal 2960 (6 lines).

Exchange Station Hotel. Owned and managed by L.M.S.R. Company.

Adelphi Hotel.—The Hotel de Luxe of the North. Porters in Uniform meet the trains at Central (Midland) Station and convey luggage to and from the Hotel free of charge. Midland Office: 21, Castle Street. Telephone: 971 Bank.

Above left: A staircase at the Adelphi Hotel, photographed on 22 April 2006. Well known for designing ships' interiors, architect Frank Atkinson gave the hotel the atmosphere of an ocean liner, and the Sefton Suite is an exact replica of the smoking lounge on the *Titanic*. Author

LIVERPOOL
AND THE
ADELPHI
HOTEL

HOTEL LMS SERVICES

Left: A 1930s LMS advertisement for the Adelphi Hotel, which became popular with passengers arriving or departing on ocean liners.

Left: A 1930s *Red Guide* note on Liverpool's railway hotels, describing the Adelphi as 'The Hotel de Luxe of the North'.

Right: A stone 'MA' (Midland Adelphi) monogram crowned with a Liver Bird, photographed in June 2007. *Author*

Left: The plasterwork in a number of the Adelphi's bedrooms, restored to their former splendour, features a garlanded 'M' (for Midland Railway). The high ceilings, marble fireplaces, huge sanitary fittings, heavily bevelled mirrors and elegant light fittings that were a prelude to the art-deco period make these rooms a veritable delight. *Author*

A Grand day out

In 1839 the Grand National, the most famous steeplechase in the world, moved to Aintree. At one time the racecourse was served by four stations. The first station called Aintree was known originally as Simonswood and was renamed Fazakerley in 1860, when the station on the Liverpool–Preston main line became the principal station for Aintree. BR later called this latter Aintree Sefton Arms, to distinguish it from the nearby ex-CLC station, by then called Aintree Central.

The fourth station, known originally as Aintree Cinder Lane, was located on the LYR's North Mersey line and was opened in 1890, purely for the Grand National. Renamed as Aintree Racecourse in 1910, when the original station of that name became Aintree Central, it was unique in that the eastbound track was set into the platform that served westbound trains. This maximised the space available (at the top of an embankment) to cope with the Grand National crowds, although eastbound trains were not admitted when the platform was in use!

The CLC station at Aintree had opened in July 1880 and at first was used only on race days. The CLC's plan to tunnel below Liverpool to reach the northern docks had proved too expensive and operationally complex, and consequently a heavily engineered and circuitous route was provided to the east of the city, via Hunt's Cross, to Huskisson and Aintree. The line originally passed through countryside, but, as this became more urbanised, additional stations were added in what became the eastern suburbs of Liverpool; these included Clubmoor (opened in 1927) and Warbreck (1929), opened to serve new council-built developments.

All lines in the area were very busy on Grand National days with special trains from all over Britain. Prior to World War 2 some 30 special trains arrived at the CLC Aintree station alone. Even the GWR ran specials to Birkenhead Woodside and then charabancs across the Mersey to the racecourse. More locally, special trains were run from nearby centres, and the LOR also ran over LYR metals to Aintree for the Grand National. The number of special trains declined postwar, with a decline in the popularity of the Grand National at that time, but six specials still ran to Aintree Central in its final year of 1963.

Regular passenger services were cut back from Aintree Central in November 1960, but the station remained in use for the Grand National until 1963. Passenger services on the surviving southern stub of this line, from Hunt's Cross to Gateacre, continued until April 1972. A siding from Fazakerley South Junction to the Metal Box Co's siding near Aintree Central Station remained open for freight until September 1968. The line from Fazakerley South

Left: The ex-CLC Aintree Central station on 14 July 1959, featuring 'Black Five' 4-6-0 No 45262 recently arrived with the 5.30pm from Liverpool Central. The station closed to regular traffic in November 1960 but remained in use for the Grand National until 1963. In 1964 it was announced that Aintree Racecourse was to be sold for development, but fortunately this did not proceed. *M. Walshaw*

Junction closed to remaining freight with the closure of the link to Huskisson, in August 1975, the lines being formally abandoned in 1979.

The Hunt's Cross–Gateacre section of line was proposed for reopening as part of the new electrified network, but this was not to be. However, the trackbed of the ex-CLC Halewood–Aintree line was used as a footpath and cycleway, known as the Liverpool Loop Line. This also forms part of the Trans Pennine Trail from Southport to Hull and itself now provides a grand day out.

The ex-LYR Aintree Racecourse station closed in March 1962, but the line remained in use until 1987 for engineering trains. Rusting and overgrown, it was formally closed in 1992, after which the track (some of which had already been stolen) was lifted. The trackbed here is now also used as a cycleway and footpath, and there are no traces of the station.

Regular passenger services over the ex-LYR link from Bootle to the excursion platforms at Aintree, ended in April 1951. Freight and special excursions continued until the 1980s, and, although singled and out of use, the remaining line was still extant in 2008, as there remains a possibility of reopening.

Red Rum's third Grand National win, in 1977, may have helped restore the popularity of the Grand National, but one of the added pleasures of the world's greatest jump race, for your author at least, was to see the excursion trains positioned in Fazakerley sidings on the North Mersey branch, thereby affording passengers (and staff) a view of the racecourse. The sidings are no more, but excursion trains, including the British Pullman train of the Venice-Simplon Orient Express and the 'Northern Belle' Pullman, still run to the Grand National, and the ex-LYR Aintree station, located opposite the racecourse entrance, remains open. A grand day out is still assured.

Below: Another view of Aintree Central on 14 July 1959, this time with Fairburn Class 4 2-6-4T No 42113 at the head of the 5pm from Manchester Central. Few passengers are apparent on the station's five platforms, deemed necessary to deal with Grand National crowds. In the background, at a higher level, can be seen the ex-LYR line to Bootle. *M. Walshaw*

Left: Although Aintree Racecourse station, along with the line from Fazakerley Junction, is no more, the bridge over the A59 road remains *in situ*, the trackbed here serving as the basis of a footpath/cycleway that forms part of the Trans-Pennine Trail. This photograph was taken in September 2006. *Author*

Left: The lines and sidings south of Aintree Central required substantial overbridges, one of which is seen here in September 2006 from the Liverpool Loop Line footpath, also part of the Trans-Pennine Trail. The ground beneath the bridge has been landscaped since closure of this ex-CLC route. *Author*

Above left: After final closure the station buildings at Aintree Central were demolished, but initially the platforms survived, being seen here derelict and overgrown in March 1969. Eventually the whole site would disappear under a new road. *N. Catford*

Left: Opened by the LYR in 1890 as Aintree Cinder Lane, Aintree Racecourse station was only ever used on race days. Heading towards Sefton Junction along the single line from the permanent-way depot at Fazakerley, Class 45 No 45 005 passes the wooden stumps (below and to the right of the locomotive) that by March 1985 were all that remained of the station. *R. Brown*

Right: A steel lattice bridge, one of two on the CLC route to Aintree that were erected in the 1930s to cross major new roads that were being constructed at the time. Photographed in September 2006, this example, which spans the A580, is now used by the footpath/cycleway known as the Liverpool Loop Line. *Author*

Above: The sizeable station building at West Derby is the only one to remain on this section of line. The station closed in 1960, and the nearby coal yard in 1964, while the line itself, having fallen out of use in 1975, was lifted in 1979. However, many features survive, and this ex-CLC trackbed, nowadays the basis of the Liverpool Loop Line footpath/cycleway, continues to provide a grand day out. *Author*

Left: A deep cutting through sandstone south of West Derby station, seen in September 2006. The bridges on this section were built in anticipation of quadrupling of the line, but traffic levels never justified this optimism, and in the final years before closure a single track sufficed. *Author*

Below: Excursions were run to Aintree CLC station by the LNER, lunch and dinner being provided on the train. Similar excursions still run today but cost rather more than the 50p charged in 1935; in 2008 a Pullman excursion from London, with lunch, dinner and a great view of the Grand National, was priced at £520 but more wonderfully was still using some of the exquisite Pullman coaches dating from the 1930s.

Right: Grand National day, 1980. Class 40 No 40 118 approaches Aintree Sefton Arms station on Saturday 29 March with a race special from London consisting entirely of First-class carriages, including two kitchen cars. Just visible in the far distance is the derelict Aintree locomotive shed. *B. Watkins*

Right: Grand National day, 1986. Class 47 No 47 571 approaches Aintree Sefton Arms on 5 April with an excursion formed of the Venice Simplon Orient Express British Pullman stock. Regular passenger services on this line had ceased in 1951, but Grand National excursions would continue until the 1990s. By 2007 the tracks that this train had travelled over from Bootle were disused and becoming increasingly overgrown, but the reopening remains a possibility. *M. Taylor*

Right: By February 2005, when this photograph was taken, the excursion platforms at Sefton Arms had fallen into disuse, excursion trains by now running only as far as Edge Hill or Lime Street, with onward connections. However, the main-line platforms used by Merseyrail trains have been modernised and improved to cope with future Grand National crowds. By the time of the author's next visit, in June 2007, the area seen here was considerably more overgrown. *Author*

21 Southport's severed services

As sea bathing and holidays became popular in Victorian times, Southport and the adjoining coast, with its sandy beaches, developed as a fashionable seaside playground. Until the 1890s Southport, known as the Paris of the North, attracted more visitors than Blackpool.

A number of railways ran to the town, and early rationalisation resulted in the first significant closure in 1860, when London Street station closed after the ELR was absorbed by the LYR. The West Lancashire Railway's Southport Central station closed in April 1901 after merger with the LYR, when trains were diverted into Chapel Street and the ex-WLR station became a goods yard.

The Southport & Cheshire Lines Extension Railway extended the CLC line some 14½ miles

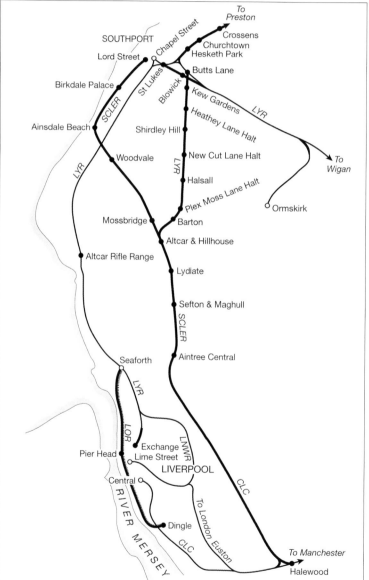

Above right: GCR 4-4-0 No 431 leaves Ainsdale Beach station just prior to World War 1. Note the wind-blown sand from the beach, by the fence on the left of the picture. This station was added after the line was opened, in an attempt to increase revenue. *Ian Allan Library*

Right: Ex-LMS Stanier Class 3 2-6-2T No 40180, showing the early BR style of numbering and livery, heads a stopping train for Liverpool Central around the 90° curve out of Southport's Lord Street station in July 1951. Passenger services would cease the following year. *W. Garth*

from Aintree to Southport and was opened in September 1884. To serve this lucrative holiday market a substantial terminus, with an imposing clock tower, was built close to the sea and fronting onto Southport's Lord Street. Its five platforms were covered with overall iron-and-glass trainsheds.

The Liverpool Central–Southport Lord Street route was 31½ miles long, compared with the 18 miles of the LYR route from Liverpool Exchange. Following electrification of the LYR line, in 1904, some expresses from Exchange took just 25 minutes, and a frequent service was provided to Southport Chapel Street. This compared with 1 hour 20 minutes to Southport Lord Street. The result was poor patronage on the SCLER route. Seaside station was added in 1901, close to sand dunes and some 3½ miles from Southport Lord Street. It was renamed Ainsdale Beach in 1911 to lessen any confusion over its location. However, an early sign of limited passenger use was apparent when stations on the line closed in 1917 as a World War 1 economy measure. The stations reopened in 1919, with the exception of the remote Mossbridge.

By the late 1930s the Southport Flower Show, established in 1924, was bringing heavy excursion traffic to the town, but in spite of this the ex-LYR Southport–Moles Cop–Altcar railmotor service, via Kew Gardens and Barton, ended in September 1938. The CLC advertised its line as 'The Pleasure Route to Southport', but passenger traffic was seasonal, being light for much of the winter period. Nevertheless, bomb damage to the ex-LYR line in

World War 2 saw heavy use of this alternative route for a time.

In 1948 the platforms at Lord Street were extended, but the Aintree–Southport section closed to passenger traffic relatively early under BR control, in January 1952, and to all traffic six months later. However, a freight siding between Aintree and Altcar & Hillhouse station remained in use until May 1960.

After closure of the Lord Street terminus at Southport the platforms were levelled, and it served as a bus station until 1987, when the trainshed was demolished and replaced by a supermarket. However, the main brick-built office part of the terminus and the clock tower remain. A considerable section of the ex-SCLER trackbed near Ainsdale has been used as the basis of a road through the attractive coastal sand dunes, while other sections are used as footpaths, notably as part of the Trans-Pennine Trail between Southport and Hull.

Direct services between Southport and Ormskirk via Burscough Junction ended in March 1962, whilst the Southport–Crossens electric service was withdrawn with closure of the line to Preston in September 1964. Through coaches to and from Euston ceased running in 1966, although for a time a DMU service was provided to/from Lime Street. Shuttle services to the railway-preservation site at Steamport ended in 1990.

Southport is still served by Chapel Street station, with frequent electric trains to Liverpool and a good service to Wigan. The Lakeside Miniature Railway and the modernised pier tramway also remain open.

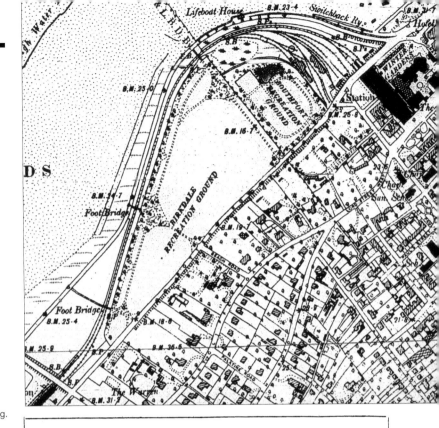

Below left: The 10.45 Liverpool Exchange–Ormskirk EMU near Aintree CLC Junction on 5 May 1966. In the foreground can be seen the termination of the ex-SCLER line at that time. The link between the SCLER and LYR here was added in 1888, mainly for the benefit of goods traffic. *I. Holt*

Right: Map of Lord Street station in 1912. *Crown Copyright*

Below right: Crossens timetable, July 1955.

Below: Crossens station on 4 July 1963, with the 10.05am from Southport Chapel Street terminating. Note the number of parcels on the platform. The electric service had been introduced in 1906 and ran some 3½ miles from Southport to Crossens. Together with the entire line from Southport St Lukes to Preston Whitehouse Junction, Crossens station would close in September 1964. The clock tower (seen here on the right) survives, although when this photograph was taken in 2006 the clock was not operational. *L. Sandler*

Table 183   **SOUTHPORT and CROSSENS—3 miles (Time on Journey 11 minutes)**

Trains call at St. Luke's 1, Meols Cop 4, Hesketh Park 6, and Churchtown 8 minutes after leaving Southport (Chapel Street).

Southport (Chapel Street) to Crossens via Meols Cop—|
On Week Days at 7 5, 7 23, 7 42, 8 9, 9 10, and 10 15 a.m.; 12 5, 12 28, 12 53, 1 10, 1 37, 2§0, 3 0, 3 49, 4 43, 5 20, 5 55, 6 15, 6 42, 10 5, 10§58, and 11£20 p.m.

Southport (Chapel Street) to Meols Cop only—
On Week Days at 6 37, 7 18, 7£50, and 9 0 a.m.; 7£15, 7§20, 10§40, 10£45, and 11£25 p.m.
On Sundays at 8 15 a.m.; 12 55, 1 5, 4 30, 6 0, 8 0, 8 35, and 10 40 p.m.

Crossens to Southport (Chapel Street) via Meols Cop—
On Week Days at 6 40, 7 24, 7 43, 8 2, 8 28, 8 43, 9 40, and 10 40 a.m.; 12 20, 12 48, 1 11, 1§30, 1£41, 1§34, 2£10, 2§16, 3 15, 4 5, 5 4, 5 12, 5 40, 6 20, 6 37 7 7, and 11§15 p.m.

Meols Cop only to Southport (Chapel Street)—
On Week Days at 6 52 and 8 19 a.m.; 12 40, 5 28, 6 20, 7£1, 9 35, 10 35, 11 0, 11£40 and 11§45 p.m.   On Sundays at 10 4 and 11 5 a.m.; 2 12, 4 7, 6 27, 7 2, 7 40, 10 10, and 10 35 p.m.

£ Except Saturdays   § Saturdays only

For **OTHER TRAINS** between Southport and Crossens, see Table 182

Table 149—

SOUTHPORT, MEOLS COP AND CROSSENS TO PRESTON

THIS PASSENGER TRAIN SERVICE BETWEEN SOUTHPORT AND PRESTON IS WITH-DRAWN, AND HESKETH PARK, CHURCHTOWN, CROSSENS, BANKS, HESKETH BANK, HOOLE, LONGTON BRIDGE, NEW LONGTON AND HUTTON AND PENWORTHAM COP LANE STATIONS ARE CLOSED.

THE AREA IS SERVED BY OMNIBUSES OPERATED BY:—

SOUTHPORT CORPORATION TRANSPORT
RIBBLE MOTOR SERVICE LTD.
PRESTON CORPORATION TRANSPORT

FOR TRAIN SERVICES BETWEEN SOUTHPORT CHAPEL STREET, ST. LUKES AND MEOLS COP, SEE TABLE 124

PASSENGERS TO AND FROM SOUTHPORT FOR THE NORTH OF ENGLAND AND SCOTLAND MAY TRAVEL VIA WIGAN WALLGATE AND WIGAN NORTH WESTERN STATIONS

Left: Notice of closure of the Southport–Crossens–Preston service in the LMR 1964/5 winter timetable.

Right: Hesketh Park station once enjoyed a regular electric service to and from Southport, but the electric conductor rails were removed after passenger closure in 1964. However, wagons could still be seen in the coal yard (right), as the station remained open for freight, from Meols Cop, until November 1967, when this view was recorded. *M. Baker*

Left: Southport Kensington Road goods depot, formerly the terminus of the West Lancashire Railway, which was absorbed by the LYR in 1897. Opened in September 1882 as Southport Central station, it became a goods depot after trains had been diverted to Chapel Street, in April 1901. Photographed in April 1965, the building would be demolished in the 1970s. *J. Clarke*

Right: St Lukes station, as it was known from 1914, with preserved L&MR 0-4-0 *Lion* passing the disused platforms on 24 March 1980. The line from Pool Hey Junction had closed to passenger traffic in June 1965, and the remaining services at this station were withdrawn in September 1968. The platforms and buildings seen here have since been demolished, but the track remains in use. *D. Eatwell*

Left: Through carriages from Euston to Southport, hauled by Fairburn 2-6-4T No 42299, pass Walton in March 1966. While Liverpool Lime Street–Alexandra Dock–Bootle local passenger services ceased in 1948, Euston–Southport Chapel Street passenger trains, running non-stop from Lime Street to Bootle, continued to use the line. The through service from Euston was withdrawn in April 1966, but in 2008 the Edge Hill–Bootle line remained open for freight. *M. Baker*

Right: Following the withdrawal in 1966 of through trains to/from Euston a replacement DMU service between Lime Street and Southport was introduced, running until May 1978. A DMU is seen on the ex-LNWR Bootle branch near Anfield on 19 April 1968. *C. Gifford*

Above: The final stretch of the line to Southport ran through a vast area of sand dunes. Much of the trackbed has been converted to a road, although the Cheshire Lines cottages at Ainsdale Beach remain and are seen here in September 2006. A new station — originally called Seaside, because of its proximity to the sea — was added in front of the cottages in 1901. In 1934 a heatwave led 100,000 to head to the coast here. *Author*

Right: The ornate brick-and-stone clock tower and entrance to Southport's Lord Street terminus, seen in April 2006. The site of the five covered platforms that were once to be found behind this frontage is now occupied by a supermarket, but a plaque informs of the history of the building. *Author*

Changing freight flows

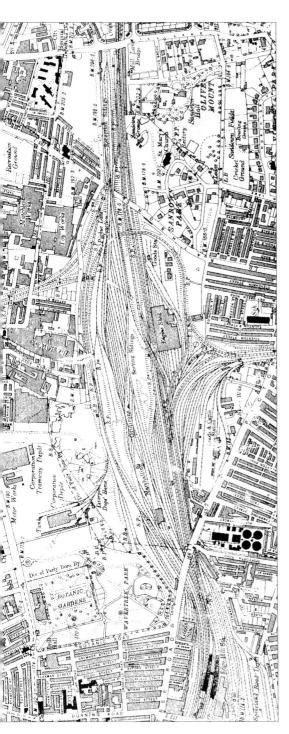

There have been many changes to Merseyside's flows of rail-borne freight, particularly to and from the docks. Cotton was important from early times, but other imports that were important to the railways included livestock and iron ore. By way of example, the Wapping depot had special facilities for handling cotton imports, while Edge Hill required a hundred horse-drawn carts to transport fruit and vegetables from the station to local markets. Exports included coal and manufactured goods. In the steam era huge quantities of these commodities were transported around the network in unfitted wagons and covered vans. The trains were marshalled in the docks and goods yards and often ran at night because of the intense operating demands on the network.

The railways also operated a diverse range of freight facilities in the area. The MD&HB dock lines apart, a whole array of lines once linked foundries, shipyards and other heavy industry, together with a plethora of goods sidings serving almost every form of freight from jam to manure. Freight offices, yards and some huge railway warehouses were also to be found throughout the area.

Congestion grew at Edge Hill as wagons were shunted between numerous sidings, and in 1873 the LNWR built inward and outward sorting and marshalling sidings, which came to be known collectively as the Gridirons, on account of the pattern created where the sidings intersected. They were also the first substantial sidings built on an incline, to allow gravity to assist with shunting and the formation of freight trains. The Gridirons were busy and at the height of freight operations employed a staff of about 100 shunters and pointsmen. A number of flyovers and underpasses were also constructed at Edge Hill to assist freight movements through the area.

The Grouping of 1923, whereby the LNWR became part of the LMS, was seen to improve freight services, but little modernisation was undertaken. The decline of rail-borne freight began after World War 2, continuing after the railways were nationalised in 1948. The 1960s and '70s saw a significant further decline in freight flows, as many individual wagonloads were lost to road haulage, and trade through the docks declined. Bananas, introduced to Britain by the Liverpool-based Elder

Left: Map of Edge Hill area in 1928, showing the many freight lines and the Gridirons. *Crown Copyright*

119

Dempster shipping line and conveyed in special vans that allowed them to ripen, constitute just one example of the many freight flows that were lost to the railways, this traffic ending in 1963.

Most local stations lost their freight services in the 1960s, while the general contraction of freight lines was mirrored at Edge Hill. The link between Olive Mount Junction and Edge Hill No 4 'box closed in 1964, the Gridirons being out of use by 1970. The Wapping goods lines closed in 1974, the Waterloo independent lines were taken out of use in 1976, the Wavertree depot was disused by 1977, and the Exhibition Junction–Wavertree link closed in July 1981. The direct spur between Edge Lane Junction and Olive Mount Junction was taken out of use in March 1987, but 20 years later there were plans to restore it.

Many of the traditional freight flows have diminished or been lost altogether, and lines, sidings and facilities have closed. Yet container and block freight has increased, prompting the establishment of container depots, the reinstatement of lines serving the north docks and the introduction of new freight services.

Left: An ex-LNWR 0-8-2T shunting a mixed goods at Edge Hill in LMS days, the differing vans and wagons giving some idea of the variety of freight at this time. In the 1870s the LNWR was already handling more than 1 million tons of freight at Liverpool each year, much of it passing through Edge Hill, and by the time of the Grouping, in 1923, this had risen to about 3½ million tons. *Eric Treacy*

Left: Shunting at Edge Hill in LMS days. Standing next to 'Jinty' 0-6-0T No 16487 are two members of the shunting staff, with poles for coupling and uncoupling the loose-fitted wagons. In the background (right), beyond Edge Hill station, can just be seen the engine house used for winding freight trains through the Wapping and Waterloo tunnels. This building remains, but Edge Hill station's overall roof has long since been demolished. *Real Photos*

Above: Edge Hill in BR days, with a long train of empty coal wagons, headed by unrebuilt 'Patriot' 4-6-0 No 45542, ready to depart for Bold Colliery, near St Helens. The colliery remained open for many years, and diesel locomotives and larger coal wagons would be used on 'merry-go-round' trains before final closure of the pit in the 1980s. *J. Carter*

Right: Framed by the Exchange viaduct's concrete pillars (which had replaced cast-iron originals damaged during World War 2), ex-LYR 'Pug' 0-4-0ST No 51206 stands at Great Howard Street on 12 November 1960. Opened in 1848, this ex-LYR goods depot would close in 1963. *J. Peden*

Left: Park Lane goods depot on 5 November 1960, with No 51206 in the distance; the structure in the foreground is one of two parallel raised running tracks that supported a gantry crane. The goods depot, which was the first to serve Liverpool docks, was opened in 1830 by the L&MR. Extensively damaged by enemy action during World War 2 but subsequently repaired, it closed to rail traffic in November 1965 but continued in use as a depot until 1972. *L. Sandler*

Left: Abandoned railway buildings remain at the old coal-wharf sidings at Edge Hill. The two-storey structures linked the sidings to a higher road level, and a walkway provided a view of the sidings. This scene was recorded in April 2006, at which time a whole range of former railway freight buildings were still to be found in the Edge Hill area. *Author*

LANCASHIRE & YORKSHIRE RAILWAY.

Goods Stations and Depots
IN
LIVERPOOL.

Great Howard Street Station.
Chief Depot for Perishables and other Goods for City Delivery.
Telephone No.: 1163.
" " 7232.

North Docks Station. ·
Depot for Goods, Cattle, and Shipment Coal.
Telephone No.: 1165.

Bankfield and Canada Docks Station.
Telephone No.: 59.

North Mersey & Alexandra Docks Station.
Telephone No.: 60.

South Docks Station.
Telephone No.: 1164.

Convenient for the undermentioned
D O C K S ;—
Victoria, Waterloo, Prince's, George's, Canning, Albert, Salthouse, King's, Wapping.

Trafalgar, Clarence, Collingwood, Salisbury, Nelson, Stanley, Bramley-Moore, Wellington, Sandon.

Canada Dock and Branches. Huskisson Dock and Branches.

Brocklebank, Carriers, Langton, Alexandra, Hornby.

Queen's, Coburg, Union, Brunswick, Toxteth, Harrington, Herculaneum.

City Office and Receiving Depot : 11, VICTORIA STREET.

All orders or communications respecting the collection or delivery of goods at any of the Liverpool Stations or Depots should be addressed to Mr. W. J. Carmichael, Goods Superintendent, Great Howard Street, Liverpool. Telegraphic Address: "PROMPTITUDE." Telephone Nos.: 1163 and 1789.

Below: Remains of the substantial walls (complete with iron tie-bar plate) of Liverpool's Park Lane goods depot, photographed in October 2006, at which time walls of a similar design were still to be found at the erstwhile Waterloo depot. Park Lane had special facilities for handling cotton, as well as large storage cellars. The latter were used for a time after the railway service ended, but by 1972 changing shipping patterns had led to the closure of all the original rail-served dockside warehouses. *R. Trill*

Right: The elegant proportions of the ex-CLC warehouse at Warrington Central. Dating from 1897, the building is of typical CLC design, with the name of the Committee's constituent companies emblazoned on the side. Large warehouses such as this were once a key feature of railway freight operations. Derelict when photographed on 19 June 1985, the building has since been converted for residential use. *L. Nixon*

Right: Designed by Henry Sumners and William Culshaw, the Midland Railway's Liverpool offices and goods store were opened in 1874 and extended four years later. This view, recorded in June 2007, gives an idea of the building's solid construction, while above the top-floor windows can be seen the city crests of Manchester, Liverpool and London. *Author*

Above: Evidence of the decline of rail-borne freight lines is to be found throughout Merseyside — a fact reflected in this June 2007 photograph taken at Kirkdale. Here the once quadruple-track ex-LYR line to Preston has been halved in capacity, such that the arch on the left of the picture now spans abandoned trackbed, while closure of the ex-CLC freight line that once linked Walton-on-the-Hill and Huskisson has rendered superfluous the twin bores further from the camera. Beneath all of this an ex-LNWR freight line still runs to Bootle. *Author*

Left: Cadbury's once conveyed its biscuits by rail, and its factory at Meols, on the Wirral peninsula, had its own shunting locomotive. Now preserved, No 14, a Hudswell Clarke 0-4-0, is seen outside the factory in October 2006. The siding to the plant was out of use by the early 1970s, but the factory itself remained active in 2007. *Author*

Left: A later pattern of rail freight developed with the Freightliner concept. Photographed on 21 October 1982, Class 47 No 47 145 heads the 14.30 departure away from the Aintree depot, since closed. The area on the right of the picture was once occupied by West End sidings, this ex-LYR line having at one time been an important route for coal to Liverpool Docks. *M. Bryan*

Right: Class 47 No 47 078 leaves Aintree Freightliner terminal on 19 January 1983. With the opening of Liverpool Freeport at Seaforth in 1984, Freightliner services would be transferred to the nearby Seaforth Freightliner terminal, resulting in the closure of the facility at Aintree. This is now an industrial area, but two of the floodlighting towers remain. *M. Bryan*

Left: A number of lines remain mothballed, facilitating their reopening should new freight flows materialise in the future. Still *in situ* at Rock Ferry is this single overgrown and rusting line to the docks at Birkenhead. Just north of here, at Green Lane, bridges leading to Woodside and the docks once provided for nine lines, emphasising the massive changes that have affected rail-borne freight over the years. *Author's collection*

23 The mighty Mersey

The origins of the world's oldest and most famous ferry service, across the Mersey from Liverpool to Birkenhead, can be traced back to the Benedictine monks of Birkenhead Priory. A steam paddle-boat service was introduced in 1815, and several routes were developed as links grew between Liverpool and the Wirral peninsula. By 1876 the Woodside Ferry alone was handling about 10 million passengers a year, an indication of the close ties between the two banks of the River Mersey.

On the Birkenhead side, William Laird built his first boiler at Wallasey Pool in 1824, thereafter joining forces with the Sheffield steel firm of Cammell to establish the famous Cammell Laird shipyard, which built the world's first iron gunboat, the first propeller steamer, the first British submarine and Britain's first welded ship. The shipyard built several ferries for railway companies and equally provided freight for Wirral's railways.

Since their inception the railways have had a close relationship with the Mersey. The GWR in particular used the ferries to gain access to Liverpool from its Birkenhead terminus, but beneath the Mersey the railway tunnel provided an alternative to the ferry from 1886. The first Mersey road tunnel opened in 1934, but it was not until 1947 that the last vehicle-carrying ferry service ran. In 1971 the second Mersey road tunnel opened, and the New Brighton ferry service ended. In 1977 the Merseyside Passenger Transport Executive tried to obtain Parliamentary consent to close the remaining ferries; it was met with national outrage, and the world-famous Mersey ferries continue today.

On the Liverpool waterfront the classically designed buildings known as the 'Three Graces' embrace the very best of early-20th-century architecture and serve as a monument to Liverpool's history as the world's premier maritime city. The Royal Liver Building, topped with the mythical Liver Birds, is the largest and most famous. For the millions who emigrated to America, or for those who were immigrants to Britain, they were as iconic to Liverpool as the Statue of Liberty was to New York; indeed the overhead railway and ferries lent the two cities some similar characteristics. Another of the 'Graces' was the headquarters of the Cunard Line, one of many shipping companies once based in Liverpool. Cunard commenced a transatlantic service from Liverpool in 1840, and the railways eventually began to play their part in providing passenger services for transatlantic travellers.

Some of the most famous ships in the world were registered in Liverpool, notably White Star's *Titanic* and Cunard's *Lusitania*, both tragically lost at sea, and the second *Mauretania*, launched from the Cammell Laird yard in 1938. The Mersey also played a pivotal role in World War 2, and the author's father was among those who sailed for North Africa on the Liverpool-registered *Aquitania*.

Just as the railways had played a key part in the development of the main Mersey docks, so they reflected their decline. In 1955 only 68 ships called at Liverpool. Cunard's last sailing to New York from Liverpool left in 1966, and as the sun set on the British Empire other passenger lines withdrew their services. Many of the docks became outdated, and the future for the Mersey looked bleak. Cammell Laird, having been a major employer engaged in vital wartime work, fell on hard times and in 1993 launched the last of 13,000 ships, although under new ownership part of the yard continues to undertake repair work.

Happily, the decline in the Mersey's trade was halted and ultimately reversed. Today many ships are once again to be seen, and a wealth of historic railway and dock structures remain, recalling Merseyside's fascinating transport history. So take advantage of the area's excellent rail and ferry services and sample the magic of the mighty Mersey.

Right: Cunard advertisement for Liverpool–New York services, April 1910. Cunard had its head office in Liverpool from 1839 until 1967.

Far right: A Liverpool Overhead Railway poster from the 1893-1908 period (when Mr Cottrell was General Manager), asserting that this was the first and fastest electric railway in the world. At the height of the dock trade more than 100 ships would be berthed at Liverpool, and the diversity of vessels that could be seen in the Mersey is clear from this poster. *Ian Allan Library*

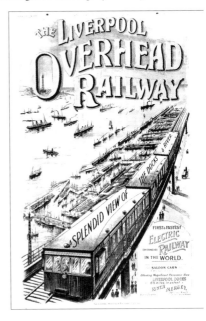

Left: The MD&HB's Riverside station in LMS days. Adjoining this large plain-roofed building is the floating Liverpool Landing Stage, which allowed ships' passengers to disembark and gain access to the station at any state of the tide. Liverpool was once Europe's foremost transatlantic port, and over the years millions of people used the docks, but the postwar era saw a dramatic decline. Riverside station closed in 1971 and was subsequently demolished. *BR*

Right: When photographed on 3 May 1927 the new rail-served warehouses at Liverpool's Gladstone Dock were almost ready for use, being officially opened by King George V on 19 July. The docks at this time were the largest in the world, and the entire complex, costing some £7.5 million, had taken more than 20 years to construct. *Ian Allan Library*

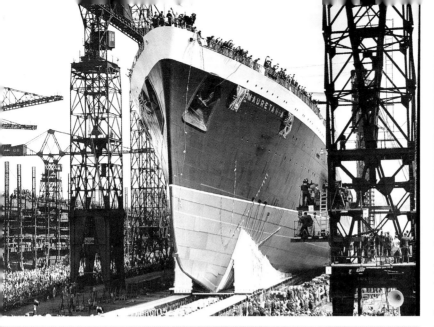

MAURETANIA TO BE SOLD FOR SCRAP

DAILY TELEGRAPH REPORTER

THE Cunard liner Maure-
tania, 35,655 tons, is to
be sold for scrap. She is
expected to fetch about £1
million, two-thirds of what
it cost to build her 26 years
ago.

In February it was forecast in
The Daily Telegraph that the
Mauretania would be withdrawn
from service in November. The
minimum of work was carried out
on her last winter overhaul in
Liverpool.

Above left: In terms of gross tonnage the largest ship ever built in England, the new Cunard liner *Mauretania* was launched from Cammell Laird's Birkenhead yard on 28 July 1938. The excitement of the huge crowd is clear, and spectators had also lined up for six miles along the Liverpool banks to watch. The Mauretania would be scrapped in 1965.
Ian Allan Library

Left: A view from the top of the Royal Liver Building of Prince's Dock and, to the north, the Liverpool dock estate. On the left is a steamer at the Liverpool Landing Stage, while on the right can be seen the LOR and the dock entrance to the Mersey Road Tunnel. The tunnel entrance survives, but almost all the buildings in the foreground, along with the LOR, have been lost since this photograph was taken on 24 June 1950.
Ian Allan Library

Below left: The world-famous ferries continue, and cruise liners are back; in this scene, recorded on 21 September 2007, the *Snowdrop* is dwarfed by the *QE2*, marking its 40th and Liverpool's 800th birthday. The following year the city would celebrate its rôle as European Capital of Culture, confirming that the tide has turned for the better on the mighty River Mersey. *Author*